Penguin Books
Cat's Cradles

A Joost Elffers and
Michael Schuyt Production

Cat's Cradles
and Other String Figures

Text by Bab Westerveld

**Translated by Plym Peters and
Tony Langham**

**Research and Explanations by
Hein Broos**

**Photography and Layout by
Mirjam de Vries**

Penguin Books

Penguin Books Ltd, Harmondsworth,
Middlesex, England
Penguin Books, 625 Madison Avenue,
New York, New York 10022, U.S.A.
Penguin Books Australia Ltd, Ringwood,
Victoria, Australia
Penguin Books Canada Ltd, 2801 John Street,
Markham, Ontario, Canada L3R 1B4
Penguin Books (N.Z.) Ltd, 182–190 Wairau Road,
Auckland 10, New Zealand

First published in West Germany by Du Mont Buchverlag GmbH & Co., as *Das Hexenspiel*, 1978
First published in Great Britain by Penguin Books 1979

Made and printed in Great Britain by
Butler & Tanner Ltd, Frome and London
Set in Times New Roman

Contents

Introduction

How to read
'front' and 'back' in
the explanatory text

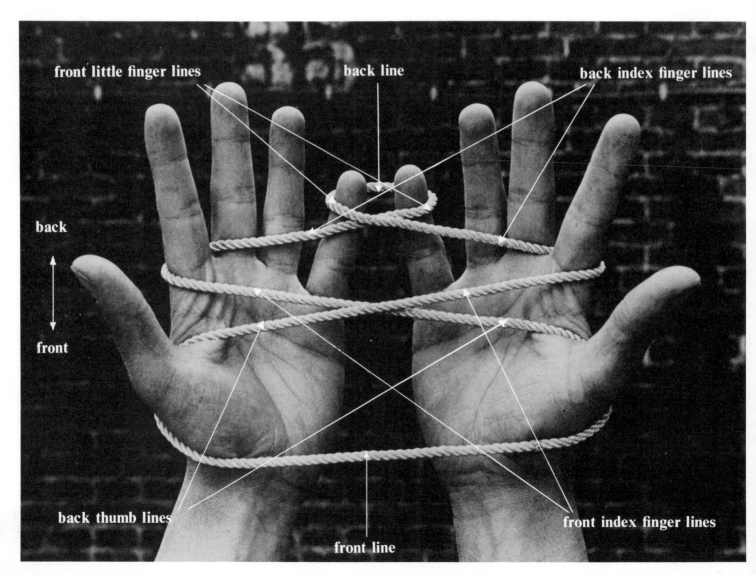

front little finger lines

back line

back index finger lines

back

front

back thumb lines

front index finger lines

front line

Your first trick

Just pick up a piece of string and within a few minutes you will be able to do your first trick. Take the string in your left hand so that a long line hangs down on either side of the hand. Show everyone that it is a closed circle of string...

Stick your right hand into the loop about half-way down. Then move round to the right, round the back line, then to your side

of the circle, to the right in front of the front line, and then right again, into the loop, under the left hand. Obviously you've tied yourself into terrible knots, but ... pull on the string with your left hand and your right hand is free again.

This trick was not thought up by someone who had been at school for ten years or even longer, but by a native of an island on the

other side of the world in the Torres Straits, near northern Australia. This native had certainly never read a book or seen a conjuror on television in his life. He simply didn't need the piece of string he happened to have on him for anything useful and so he played with it. Not for any particular purpose, but just for fun. This book is about playing and the fun you can have.

Two girls playing cat's cradle. A nineteenth-century engraving.

Why not make your imagination work?

It's a very strange phenomenon really. The Chinese have tangram – five triangles, a rhomboid and a square – and with these they can make almost anything you can think of; the Japanese have origami and they can fold a piece of paper into anything at all; Indians, Eskimos, Papuans and many other races have string games and use string to express everything that they see around them. But what do we have? Our grandmothers secretly used to play Cat's Cradle under the desk at school; some mothers might still know The Cup and Saucer and possibly even The Smith's Secret, but that's about the extent of their knowledge.

Can't we enjoy ourselves with a piece of paper, a length of string or a few blocks of wood, even though they hardly cost anything? We ought to try because games stimulate the imagination and give you new ideas, as you can see by looking through this book.

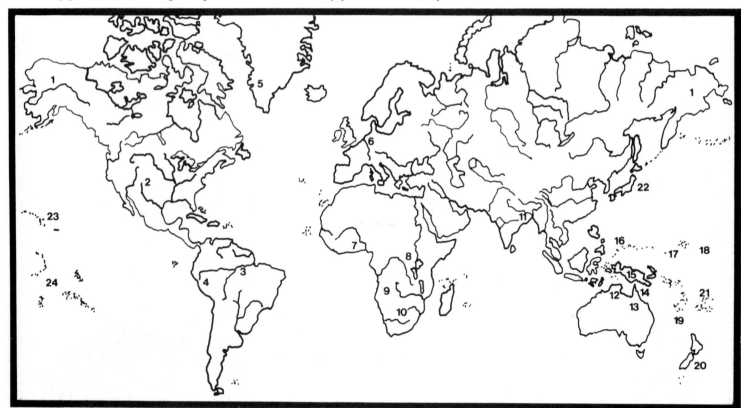

Where do string figures come from?

1. **Alaska, eastern Siberia**
2. **North America**
3. **The Guianas**
4. **Peru**
5. **Greenland**
6. **Western Europe**
7. **Mali, Zanzibar, Sierra Leone**
8. **Central Africa**
9. **Angola, Botswana**
10. **Rhodesia, South Africa**
11. **Bengal**
12. **Arnhem Land**
13. **Queensland**
14. **Torres Straits**
15. **New Guinea (Papuas)**
16. **Palau Islands**
17. **Nauru**
18. **Gilbert Islands**
19. **New Caledonia**
20. **New Zealand**
21. **Fiji**
22. **Japan, Korea, China**
23. **Hawaii**
24. **Marquesas, Society Islands**

String figures?
Never heard of them!

At the end of the last century an English anthropologist suggested that games might prove very useful in his work, because people are truly themselves when they play games, and in string figures they can clearly express their attitudes to their environment, their thoughts and their customs. In 1888 an American, Franz Boas, made the first careful attempt to describe how Eskimos made their string figures. This encouraged anthropologists to spread far and wide in their quest for knowledge; the islands of the South Seas, Australia, New Zealand and other islands were particular favourites for research. (Africa was practically ignored.) These anthropologists must have been surprised, as someone would be who has never seen a piano and then suddenly hears a pianist making music with his fingers. The natives were not actually waiting for them with a piece of string at the ready; in fact, if they were playing a game, for example, seeing who could make The Paths to the Well the quickest, they would not be particularly keen on having a stranger standing around watching them. For that matter, it would be difficult for someone who had played the piano all his life to talk about music to someone who had never seen a piano and could not even play a scale on the white keys. Sometimes anthropologists asked for help from local missionaries in case they knew a little more about string figures, but in most cases they had never heard of them.

J. Andersen studies a string figure.
Alexander Turnbull Library, Wellington, New Zealand.
Photograph from Pieter van Delft's collection.

Woman from the Tahu tribe shows string
figures to the anthropologists D. Elsdon Best
and J. Andersen (wearing the cap).

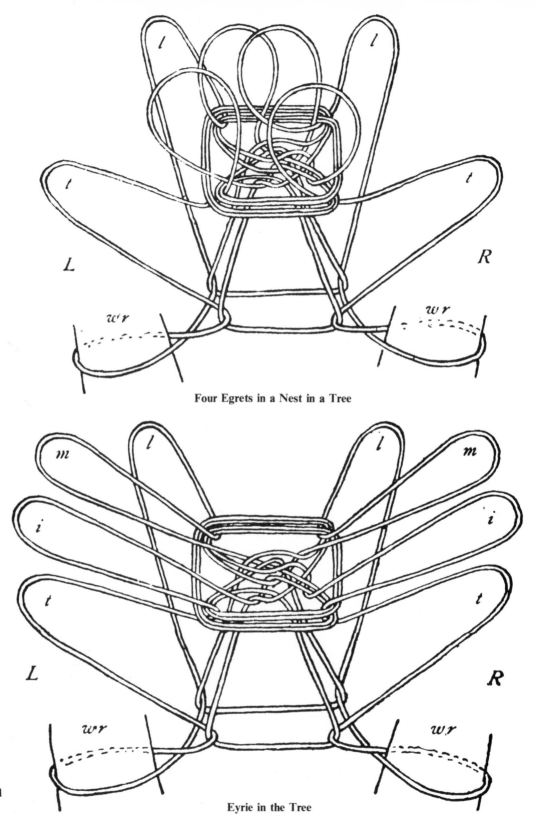

Four Egrets in a Nest in a Tree

Eyrie in the Tree

Illustrations from articles by
W. Roth in 'North Queensland
Ethnography', 1902.

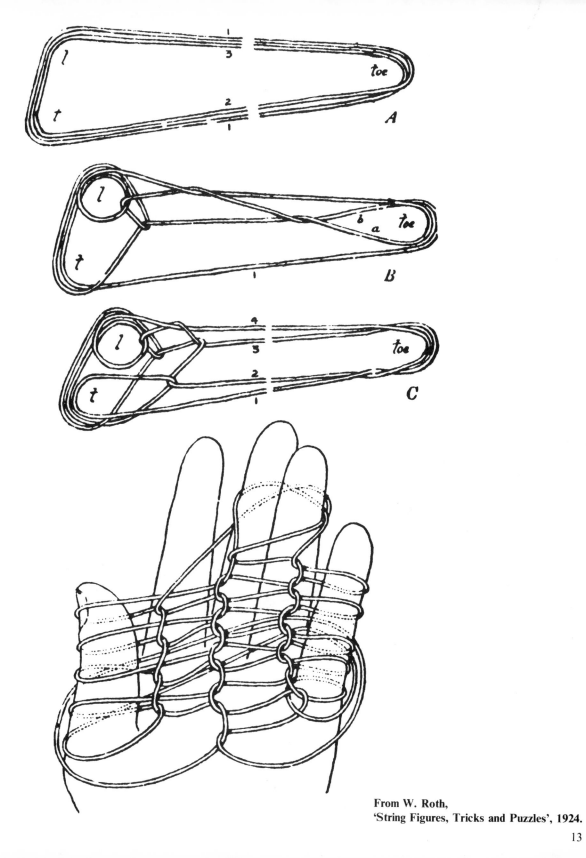

From W. Roth,
'String Figures, Tricks and Puzzles', 1924.

The magic of string

It's not really surprising to learn that most missionaries did not understand string figures. In the cultures we think of as 'primitive', string figures were often much more than a mere game; they had magical powers and were used in funeral ceremonies and other religious rituals. On the Gilbert Islands for example, Ububwe was the god of the string figure and before entering the hereafter everyone was questioned by him on their knowledge of cat's cradles. But he was certainly not a solemn deity; the children of the islands played guessing games with their pieces of string in which they had to guess which god would be represented in the next figure. The Eskimos also believed that string figures had magical powers; when the dark, cold winter of the North Pole was approaching they would make a string sun to catch the real sun.

All in all, missionaries were not likely to be popular guests when string games were being played.

Illustration from 'The Central Eskimo', an article by Franz Boas, Washington, 1888.

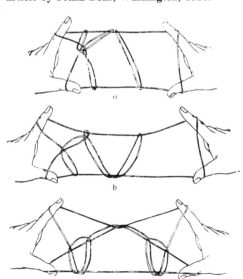

A pocketful of string

Nevertheless, some anthropologists managed to make contact with the string experts through the medium of string itself. Real *aficionados* of the game like the Englishmen, Haddon and Rivers, were accepted as friends into the string circle and in 1902 Haddon published about thirty figures which he had seen on the islands in the Torres Straits. It is not difficult to imagine how much patience was required; the man making the figure – which normally took just a few seconds to complete – had to repeat it in slow motion ten or even twenty times, and Haddon had to note it down movement by movement. He made copious notes and developed a terminology reminiscent of obscure Latin texts, incredibly precise and extremely boring to follow. Nevertheless, he showed the way for the many who followed. In 1910 the current joke about anthropologists was that they were people with their pockets full of string.

A proa (Malay vessel).
An illustration from Roth's articles, 1902.

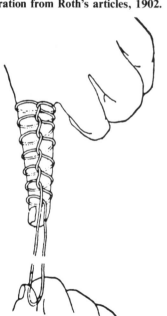

Not reading but dancing

Haddon's experiences will be quite familiar to anyone who knows a few string figures already. (After a little practice they are quite easy to master.) He wrote down every step as meticulously as a composer notates his music. But even the best composer cannot tell the pianist how to move his wrists, his hands, his fingertips and arms for each separate note – he would have to put it all down in a long, boring book that no one would ever read. Fortunately this isn't necessary. The way in which the fingers dance, the rhythm of movement is within you, and that is what 'playing' is all about. This is equally true of string games. Very soon you notice that your fingers start to 'remember' movements far faster than your eyes can read. After just a few exercises they will dance ahead of the words.

A string game with the nose.
From 'Jeux Dogons'.

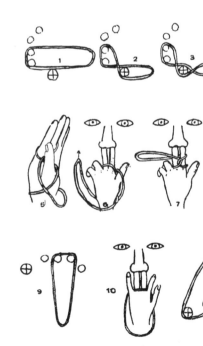

People all over the world

The invention of the string game

Anthropologists had another reason for being enthusiastic about string games. They discovered that Red Indians were making figures that had also been found in the South Sea Islands, thousands of miles away; they immediately came to the conclusion that this was the long-sought-after proof for all kinds of population migration. They no longer believe in this theory; gradually they realized that some games, especially simple, playful games, were common to people all over the world, throughout the ages. It's quite possible that The Escaping Lizard, the first trick in this book, could be found in a dozen other places as well. Anyone who takes a piece of string to tie up a parcel could begin to play with it. They could be expressing something or just playing, thinking something over, entertaining other people or illustrating a story to symbolize the invisible and make it real.

It's always easy to find a piece of string.

According to the people of Arnhem Land the first people to make rope and string were Wawalik and Mudawa. They lived on the Bay of Buckingham.

The story of Maidka-uma (a fragment)
'... In Jelganoe a koes-koes crossed their path. They killed it, took out its innards and used the intestines to make a figure of a koes-koes. They found an eyrie with a young egret in Gumuiumir. They took it out of the nest, laid it down on the ground with its wings spread out and made a string figure of it. In Magalmagul they saw a kiwi walking about. They took a good look at the bird, made some magical tying loops round their fingers and the bird was immortalized in string. In Garajamga they ventured into the jungle. They dug up a few potatoes; the eldest girl passed them to her sister and made a string figure of them. Then she looked between her sister's legs and made another string figure of what she saw there. The younger sister turned her back in shame but then her sister made a string figure of her whole body, including her shoulder-bag. They continued on their way and found another potato in the ground. This time they boiled it and the eldest sister divided it up equally with a shell. This time the youngest made a string figure of it. When they arrived in Burrannina they made a string figure of a wallaby and in Ilganu they found an emu's eggs. After this they saw the emu itself and later an even bigger emu. They made string figures of all these things.

A Tortoise Shell.
An illustration from Roth's plate 7 in 'North Queensland Ethnography', 1902.

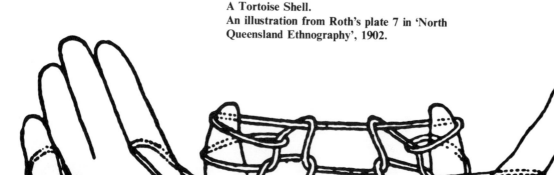

They continued on their way; in Gadina they made various string figures of a wauraan, in Karardina of a caterpillar, and in Burunbura of a snake. On the way they saw a brace of ducks in the lagoon at Waimijunga but they dived into the water when the girls passed so they made a string figure of dabbling ducks and of the lagoon. They also discovered a water-lizard and made two figures of it; the water and the lizard. They also made figures of the tortoise they saw there. At Gulawuna they went back into the jungle where they saw a flying fox which flew into a treetop; they made figures of the flying fox and the treetop. They ended up in the Milnardji marshes and picked some rakias; the youngest girl put the bulbs in her hand and her older sister made the string figure. Then the youngest laid a fire. They baked the bulbs in the hot ashes and pressed the baked bulbs into a cake. Before they had finished eating it, one of the sisters had made a string figure of it. They saw many other things in the marshes: a bloodsucker, a yellow needle-fish, and a catfish and they made string figures of all these things. The oldest girl made a net to fish with and the youngest made a string figure of the net and the fish. They came to Guluana where they saw a tree which gives ironwood and they made a figure from the resin. Then they made one of a stickleback and a young thornback and finally a whole series of a stilt-bird.'

Once you start, there's no stopping.

Maori children displaying their string skills.
Alexander Turnbull Library, Wellington,
New Zealand.
Photograph from Pieter van Delft's collection.

16

Who plays who?

Girls play with girls, boys with boys amongst the Yirrkalla people of northern Australia – at least in string games. The girls learn female figures from their mothers; the boys learn male figures from their fathers, and no one is allowed to spy on the opposite sex. A boy who makes a female figure gets a clip round the ear.

Women only play with their string when they are together. There is hardly ever a man around. And when there happens to be a man near by he pretends not to see anything – he considers it women's business.

However, there are exceptions to this rule; it's a question of knowing what they are. A man who gives a hand (or two) with a string figure must either be a very good friend or a close relative. It's no simple matter to find out who is allowed to help a woman. Her *nabibi* (mother's brother) may, but her *nadjiwalga* (great-grandmother's brother's son) may not. Her *maralgoe* (grandmother's brother's son) may, but her *gurong* (father's sister's daughter's son) may not. Her *gadu* (son) may of course help her, but her *galle* (mother's brother's son) may not. Life is not easy for a Yirrkalla woman.

Left: Surinam children playing cat's cradle at school in Amsterdam.

Right: The Elastic Twist, played by children at the Montessori School in Amsterdam.

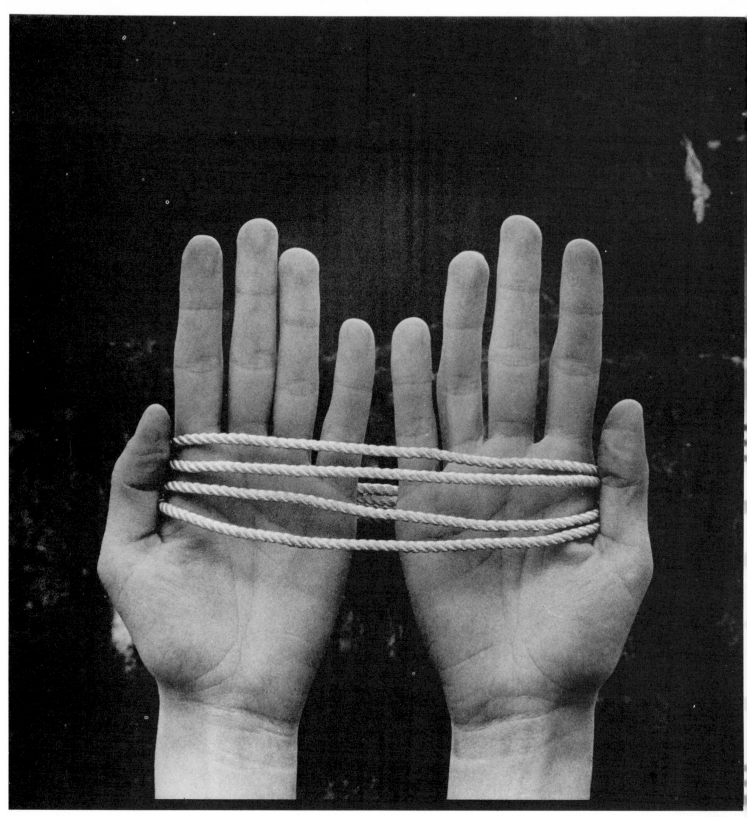

The string circle

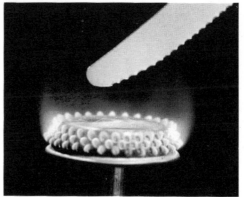

Heat up a knife,

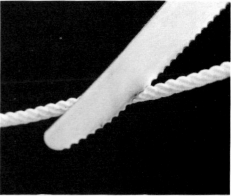

cut the string,

heat up the two ends

and press them against each other.

What sort of string to use

String is string but not every sort is suitable for using to make string figures. Eskimos used plaited reindeer fibres or sealskin which was cut into thin strips. In other places they made 'vegetarian' string from plant fibres, as we do from hemp, for example. In Australia women grew their hair long and when they needed string they cut and plaited it. They also used the strong sinews from a kangaroo's hind legs as this was fine for making string figures.

Now that all these species are threatened with extinction it is best to leave them alone and use some other material, but not thin twine or packing string as this can cut into the fingers, nor a piece of wool, because it will get tied in knots.

A length of cord made of plaited cotton about the thickness of a knitting needle makes the best 'string', but a plaited or

Fisherman's knot

Reef knot

beaten length of nylon cord is also very suitable and is available from almost any hardware or furniture shop or a shop that sells sailing accessories. These sorts of string are easy to disentangle because they do not fluff. This is very important for complicated figures.

The length

You can make most figures with a piece of string two metres long. For some figures you will need a shorter piece of string but you can always double up the string circle. To make the most complicated figures it is best to use a longer, thinner cord.

How to make a circle

If you have chosen a cotton cord, tie a strong knot (a reef knot or a fisherman's knot) – shown on the left – to make a circle. Pull hard on the knot and snip the ends. If you have chosen nylon cord it will take a while before it is nice and supple. It is better not to tie a knot as it will invariably fray. You can join the two ends by melting them with a soldering iron. As you can see from the photographs, it is also possible to do it at home. Cut the cord to the desired length and heat up a knife in the flame of a gas cooker. Heat up the ends of the cord with the knife until they melt and then join the two ends so that they fuse. This gives you a strong string circle without a knot; this works very well. However, nylon cord can be rather awkward for complicated figures. The best thing for these is a cotton cord consisting of a centre with threads woven round it carefully.

Bind off the ends with thread or silk and then use the same thread to sew the ends together.

A final hint

When a figure is completed and you want to pull it out, it is important to pull on the right line if you want to avoid ending up with a dreadfully tangled knot. Pulling the figure upwards and downwards from the middle usually works.

When a figure involves having a second loop on a single finger it is important to keep this on top of the other one unless specifically stated otherwise.

When you look at the photographs and compare them with the figures on your own hands there is always one big difference; on the photographs you see the palms of the hands. We have done this for the sake of clarity to enable you to see exactly how the lines go.

First learn how to start

First position 1

– Lay the string circle behind the thumbs, in front of the palms and behind the little fingers of both hands. Make sure that the long lines are parallel.

First position 2

– Lay the string circle around both index fingers. (For some figures another finger is indicated.)
– Put the thumbs through the two lines from below.

– Move the thumbs down and away from you from below, and up and towards you, so that there are loops around the thumbs and index fingers.

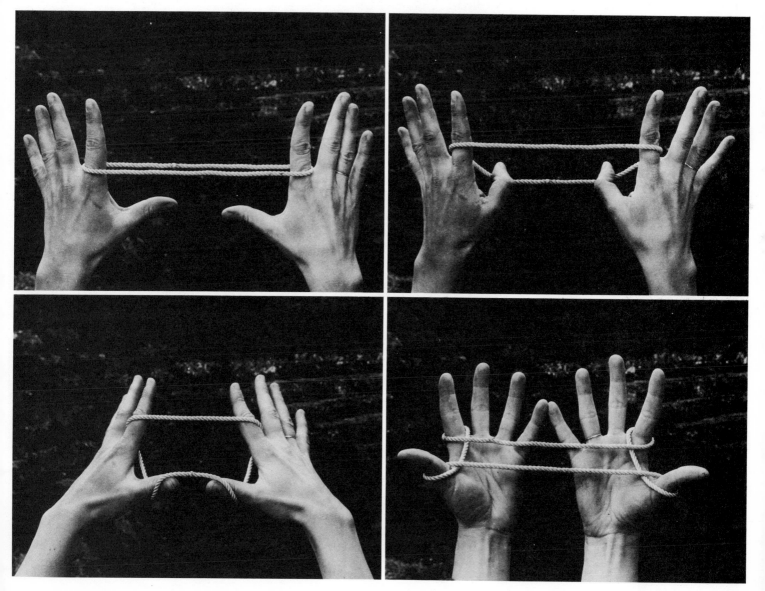

Opening A

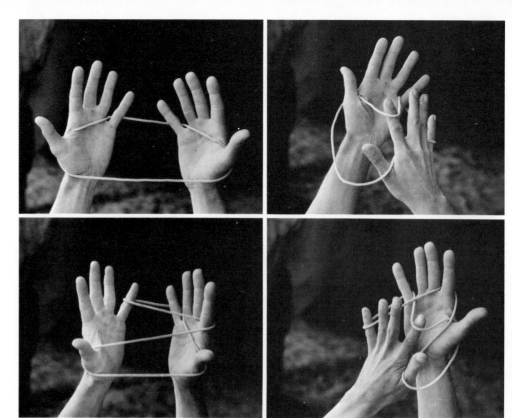

An opening you need to know like the back of your hand, as it is used in many string figures amongst the Eskimos, the Indians of North and South America, as well as amongst the Papuans. Most of the figures in this book start with this opening.

– Do first position 1 (see page 22).

– Stretch your hands and from below put the right index finger behind the line which runs across the left palm. Pull the cord tight.

– From below, put the left index finger behind the line which runs across the right palm between the two lines which come from behind the right index finger. Again pull tight.

– Make sure that you do this in the correct order, i.e. first right, then left.

The Murray opening

First variation

- Lay the string circle around both index fingers.
- Take the back line between the thumbs and index fingers of both hands about half-way, keeping about 12 cm of string between them.
- Bring the hands close together so that the string crosses over and there is a standing loop above the crossover.
- Take hold of this loop on either side with the thumb and middle finger of both hands.
- Put both index fingers through the loop from the front, let the thumb and middle finger go, so that the loop is hanging from the index fingers. Then pull the string tight with the index fingers.
- Keep the lines on the index fingers completely separated: there should be two parallel lines in front of the index fingers and two crossed lines behind them.

Second variation

- Take the string circle by the thumb and middle fingers of both hands keeping about 12 cm of string between them.
- Bring the hands together so that the string crosses over and there is a loop hanging beneath the crossover, right over left.
- From above, put both index fingers in the back of the loop, then turn them towards you and up. Pull the string tight with the index fingers.

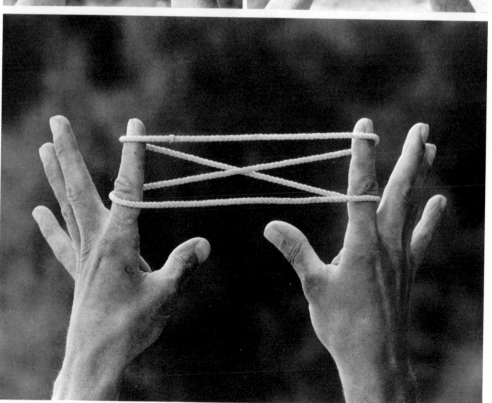

The ribcage opening

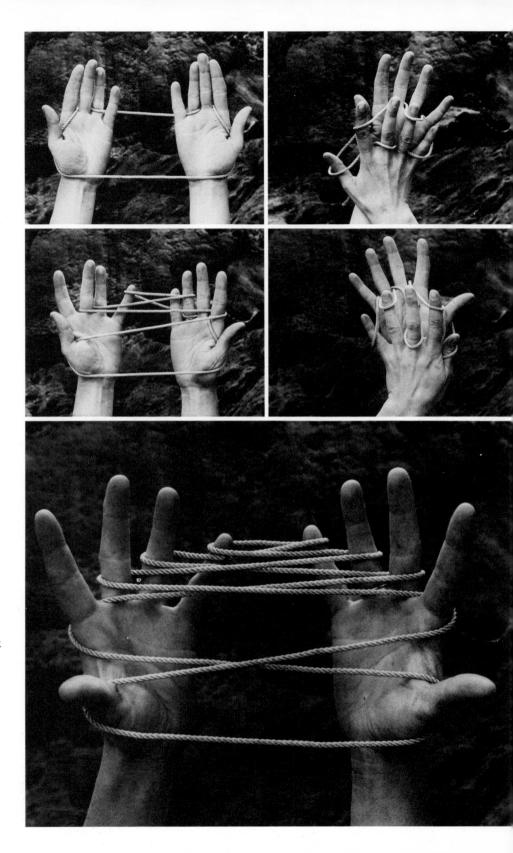

First variation
– Do the first position 1 (see page 22).
– With your right hand put the line running across the left palm behind the left middle finger. Do the same for the right hand.
– From below, put the right index finger behind the line which runs in front of the left index finger and do the same with the right ring finger to the line in front of the left ring finger. Pull the string tight.
– Do the same for the right hand with the index and ring fingers of the left hand making sure you stay inside the lines on either side of the relevant fingers. Pull the string tight.

Second variation
– Do the first position 1 (see page 22).
– From below, place the index and ring fingers of the right hand behind the line running across the left palm. Pull the string tight.
– Do the same for the right hand with the index and ring fingers of the left hand (staying within the lines).
– From below, put the middle finger of the right hand behind the line running in front of the left middle finger. Pull the string tight again and do the same for the right hand (making sure that you stay within the lines which come from behind the right middle finger).

Third variation
– Do opening A (see page 24).
– Bend the ring fingers under the back index finger lines and straighten them out again.
– From below, put the right middle finger behind the line running in front of the left middle finger (exactly as in the second variation). Pull the string taut and do the same for the right hand with the left middle finger.

Opening for Cat's Cradle

– Lay the string circle around the wrists.
– Wind the string once round the wrists on either side (making sure that the long lines remain parallel).
– From below, put the right index finger behind the line in front of the left wrist, and pull the string tight. Do the same to the left wrist with the left index finger. (Stay within the lines coming from behind the right index finger.)

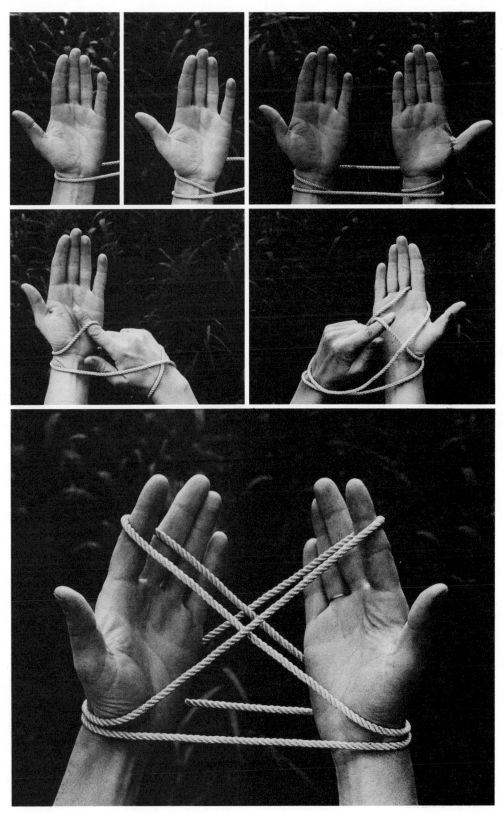

The Navaho opening

This opening gets its name from the fact that it was first seen amongst the Navaho Indians.
- Take the string circle between the thumb and index finger of both hands, leaving about 12 cm of string between them.
- Bring the hands together so that the string crosses over with a loop hanging down under the crossover.
- Put both index fingers through the loop from behind, supporting the string with the other fingers.
- Turn the index fingers down and then up and away from you so that the small loop hangs on the index fingers while the thumbs are holding the large loop. Pull the string taut.

The Pindiki stroke

On the Polynesian Islands there is a large number of figures – many of which are described in this book – that completely unfold with the final movement. The whole hand is involved in this movement – the Pindiki stroke. This example, The Kiwi (which is shown on page 93), ends as follows:

You press the thumbs against the index fingers so that no lines can escape. Then you bend the index fingers under the line indicated. Now turn your palms towards you and lift this line with the tips of your index fingers. Turn your palms away so that the line makes a half-turn around the top of the index fingers, and at the same time press the back lines against the palms with the other fingers.

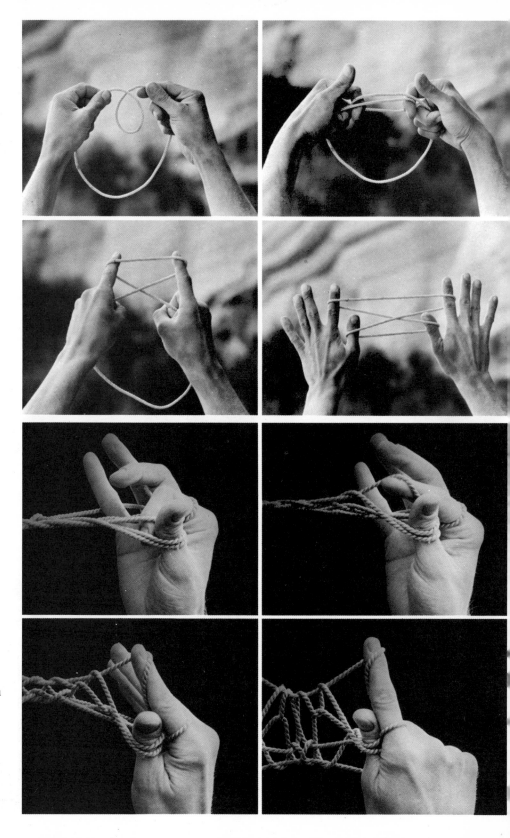

The turning stroke

The turning stroke is another common final movement used to unfold a figure. This example shows the Two Diamonds (see page 49).

Having arrived at the eighth intermediary position (illustration 1) of Two Diamonds, put your index fingers into the triangles next to the thumbs from above (illustration 2), simultaneously freeing the little fingers (illustration 3). Then you spread the thumbs and index fingers (illustration 4), at the same time turning the palms of the hands down and outwards (illustration 5).

The higher the loops are on the thumb and index finger, the better the figure unfolds.

The Navaho leap

On the right we show three ways in which the Navaho Indians make a loop leap over another loop above it, whether it's on the same finger and goes over that finger or whether it is taken over the whole hand. It is then dropped.

Example 1: the thumb and index finger of one hand lift the bottom loop over the top one and over a finger of the other hand (illustrations 1, 2, and 3).

Example 2: you turn the thumbs in and downwards, the loop jumps over it and the thumbs come up again (illustrations 4, 5, and 6).

Example 3: the teeth do the job, instead of the thumb and index finger as shown in the first example (illustrations 7 and 8).

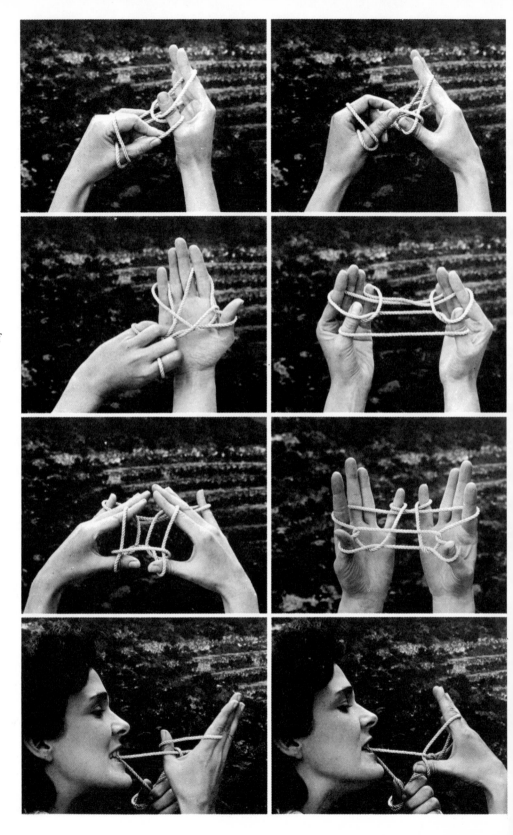

Take the first figure
The Cup and Saucer

Almost everyone in western Europe knows The Cup and Saucer though few people know that the figure probably originated in New Caledonia.
– Do opening A (see page 24).
– Bend the thumbs over the crossed lines at the front, put them in the second cross from below and pull the back index finger lines on the thumbs towards you.
– Do a Navaho leap over both thumbs (see page 30) with the bottom thumb line.
– Free the little fingers and move the hands away from each other, spreading the thumbs and index fingers.

The Salish Indians on the west coast of Canada also knew this figure but obviously had a different name for it: Skinning the Bison. They also made the figure in a different way.
– Do opening A (see page 24).
– Free the little fingers without pulling the other lines tight.
– Throw the hanging back line forwards between the hands and over the other lines.
– Take this line from above with bent thumbs and pull downwards between the two thumb lines. Stretch out the string with spread thumbs and index fingers and the beast is skinned.

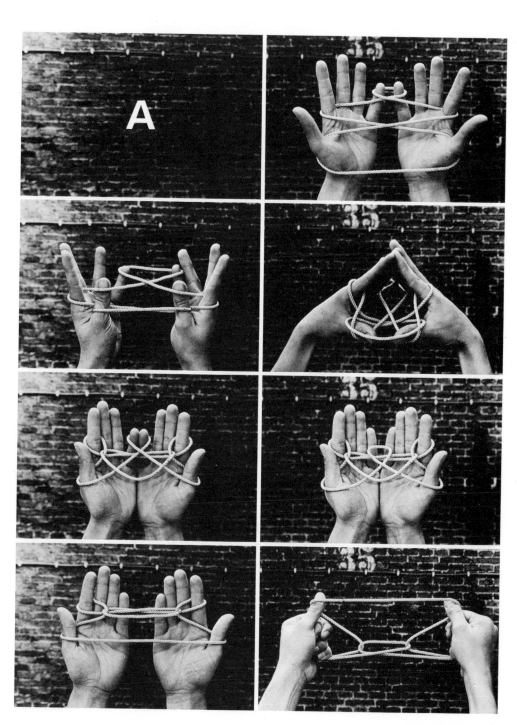

The Cup and Saucer

The Eiffel Tower

A whole series of very simple, enjoyable figures is derived from The Cup and Saucer.
– Take the straight line which links the thumbs between the teeth, free the thumbs, pull the whole figure downwards with the index fingers and you see The Eiffel Tower.
– Move the index fingers to the side and slide the knot half-way along, about a hand's breadth down from the mouth, and you have The Coat-hanger.
– Drop the loop from the mouth, and hanging down there is A Sock on the Line.

The Coat-hanger

A Sock on the Line

String Around Your Neck and Pull

A trick that is known almost all over the world and is successful every time.
– Lay the string circle around your neck.
– Take hold of the right line with the right hand and wind it once more round your neck from the front.
– Make a loop by laying the left line of the hanging loop over the right line. (The loop must be big enough for your head to pass through easily.)
– With the hands, take hold of this loop at the crossover, put your head through the bottom loop and put the crossover of the string at the back of your neck.
– Pull the loop hanging on your chest with a jerk and the string should be in your hand.

The Chicken Bum

This figure was found in many places throughout the world during the twenties: in the Guianas, Peru, Sierra Leone, as well as in Hawaii, where it was known as The Wink. A simple figure but a very intriguing one, as it moves.

– Hang the string circle round the index finger and the middle finger of one hand.

– Take the line which comes from behind the middle finger and loop it once more round both fingers. Lay it between the thumb and index finger behind the thumb.

– Pull out the loop that has been forced down a little and stick in the thumb from below.

– Lay the line hanging across the palm of the hand over the three lines, between the thumb and the index finger, behind the thumb, and bring the line which was hanging there already back between the thumb and index finger and over the lines.

– Slide the loops to the tops of the fingers and the thumb and pull on the lines which are hanging down, spread the fingers, pull, spread, etc., with rhythmic movements.

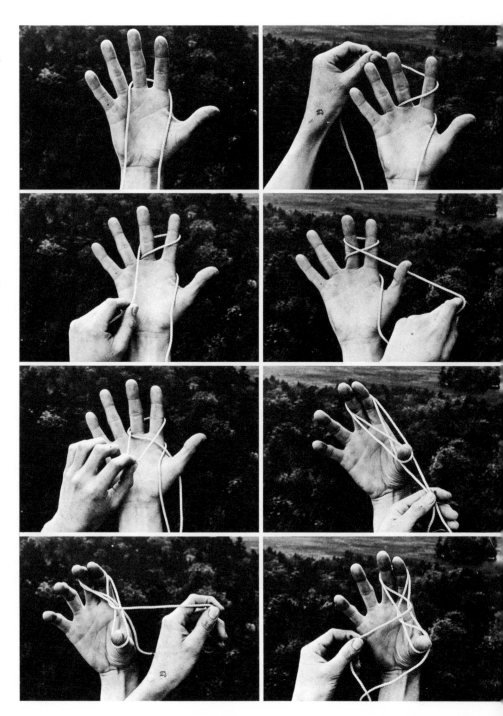

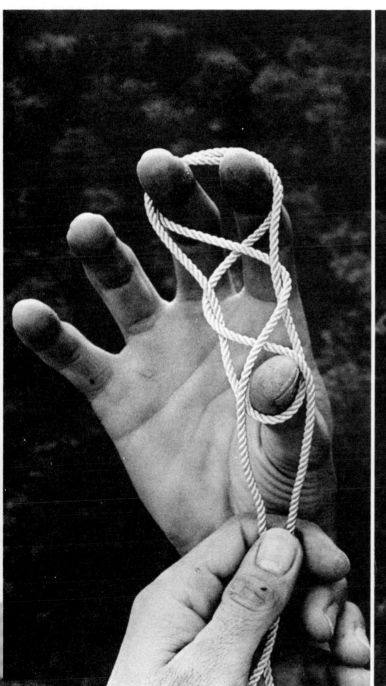

The Monkey Bum

This is another moving figure that is fun to make. It comes from the Guianan Indians and is also known as The Flying Parrot.

– Hold the string circle between the index finger and middle finger of the left hand in such a way that there is a large loop across the palm of the hand and a small loop over the back.

– Bring the small loop over the two fingers with one line to the left of the index finger and one to the right of the middle finger.

– Do a half-turn with this loop and lay it around the index and middle fingers.

– Pull the small double loop formed in this way down on to the ball of the thumb.

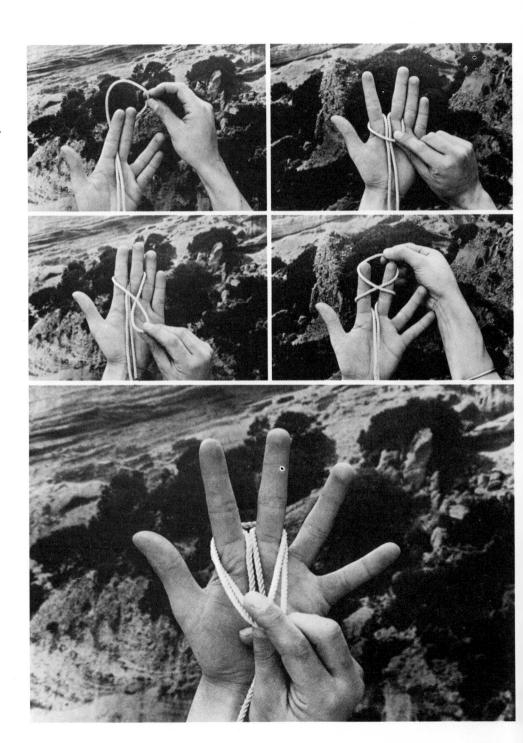

- Take the left line of the large loop through the small loop and lay it around the thumb. Do the same with the right line, this time around the little finger.
- Take the small loop behind the index finger and middle finger and pull it over the two fingers to the front.
- Slide the loops up the fingers towards the tips and then spread the hand.
- Pull on the large loop, spread the fingers, pull and spread the fingers again, with a rhythmic movement.

The Thumb-catcher

A piece of string is a marvellous thing for making figures but it can also be used to do very easy baffling tricks. This one is always a great success.

– Do the first position 1 (see page 22) but change the string round on one hand in such a way that the lines between the hands cross over. (The line from left front to right back should be on top.)

– Do opening A (see page 24), beginning with the right index finger.

– Bend the thumbs over the front crossed lines. Press down and turn right through towards you and up.

– Free the index fingers and little fingers.

– Move the hands away from each other – the thumbs are tied.

The Fly

This is a simple trick that makes a big impression. It is known all over the world under many different names including The Mosquito and Smashing a Coconut. The trick is in the tail.

– Lay the string circle around the thumbs.

– With your right hand lay both lines behind the left hand away from you.

– From above, hook the right little finger

ound the double line behind the left hand nd pull it between the index finger and humb of the left hand. (The double line tays behind the left hand.)
- With the left little finger take the two lines o the right thumb over the other four lines.
- With the right hand lift the double line

from behind the left hand over this hand and drop it.
– Pull on the knot in the middle and you will see the fly between your hands.
– Clap your hands, sliding the loops off the little fingers at the same time. Pull the string tight and the fly disappears.

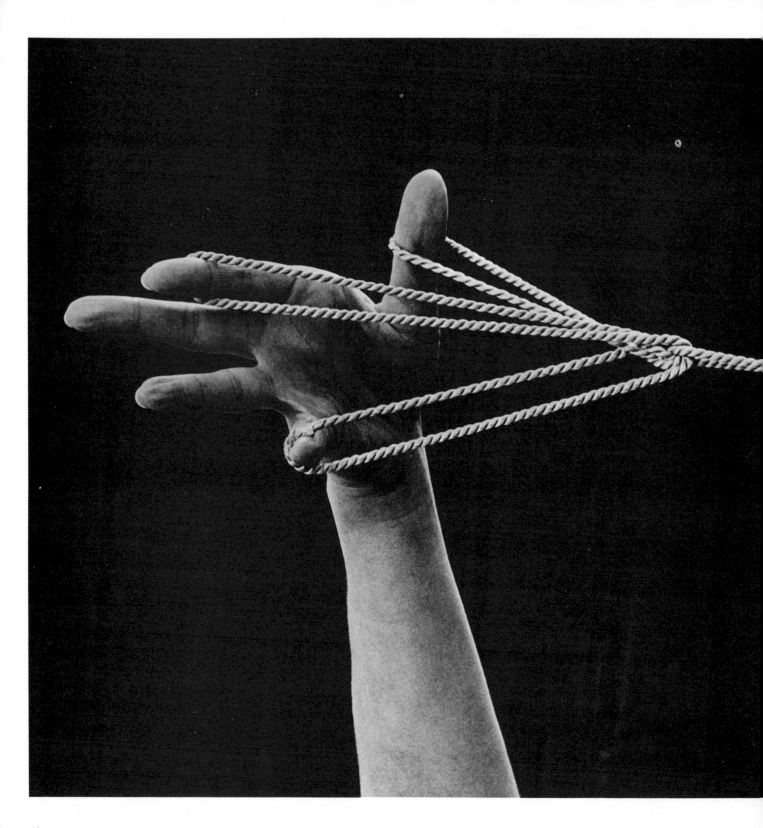

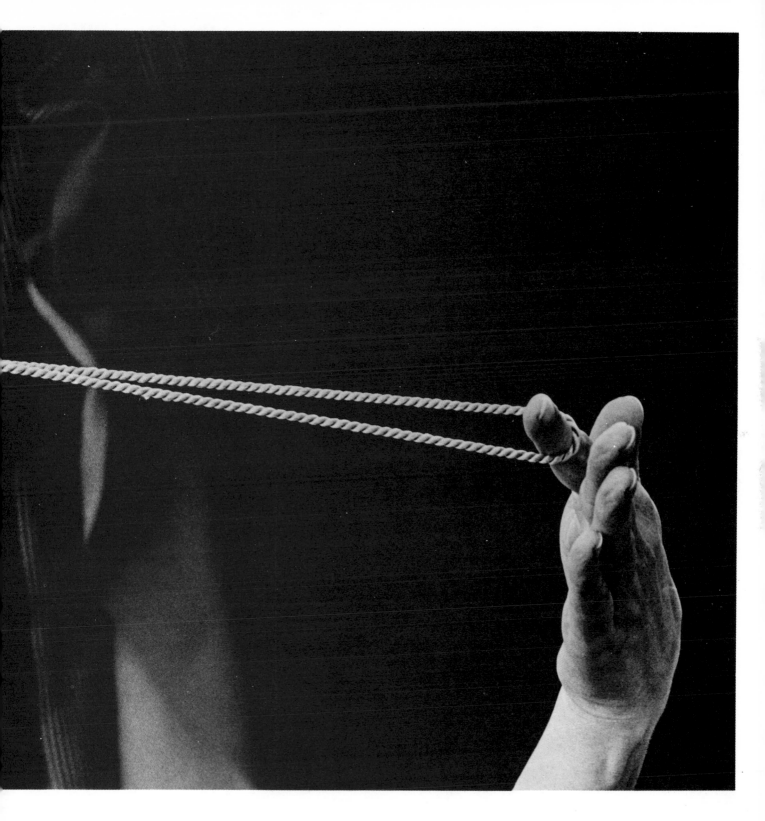

The Parachute

This fairly simple figure originates from a time when man had no concept of aeroplanes or parachutes – he was still fishing with a spear and therefore saw a fishing spear in this figure.

– Do first position 1 (see page 22).
– From below, put the top of the right index finger behind the line running across the left palm, pull the string taut, and make a double turn in the two lines with the top of the index finger. (Keep the string taut or it will slip off the fingers.)
– Let the loop slide down the right index finger and pull the line across the right palm through it from below with the left index finger. Then pull the string taut.
– Free the thumb and little finger of the right hand and pull the string taut. Vertically it looks like a parachute; horizontally like a fishing spear (see pages 40–41).

The Smith's Secret 1

This trick probably originates in Europe and has spread from there across the whole world. We discovered it in a Dutch physics textbook dating from 1869.

palm: again the line of the index finger should be on top. Pass the top line between the index finger and middle finger and the bottom line between the ring finger and little finger. Let the loop hang down under the hand.
– Pass the left line of the hanging loop between the thumb and index finger and lay it on the palm. The long loop should now be hanging to the right of the hand.

– Hang the string circle over the palm of the left hand which should be face up.
– Pull the left line of the loop hanging under the hand between the index finger and middle finger, and the right line between the ring finger and little finger.
– Take hold of the double loop again, pull it through the index finger and thumb, then in front of the thumb, and divide it in front of the

– Pull out the double thumb loop so that the string is taut, and free the thumb. You should now have a double long loop in your hand.
– Pull the double left line of the loop between the index finger and the middle finger and the right line between the ring finger and little finger. Let go of the loop.
– Pull on the line running across the palm of the hand and you will discover the smith's secret.

The Mouse

This game is known literally all over the world, amongst the Eskimos, the Indians of North and South America, in Japan, on the Philippines and in Australia. It is known by many different names. We commonly call it The Smith's Secret.

– Put your left hand up, with the palm of the hand towards you and the fingers pointing to the right. Lay the string circle over the thumb with one line in front and one behind the hand.

– Put the right index finger to the left of the front line, between the index finger and the thumb, hook the tip of the finger over the back line, pull it towards you, make half a turn with the fingertip, clockwise, so that you make a loop and lay it around the index

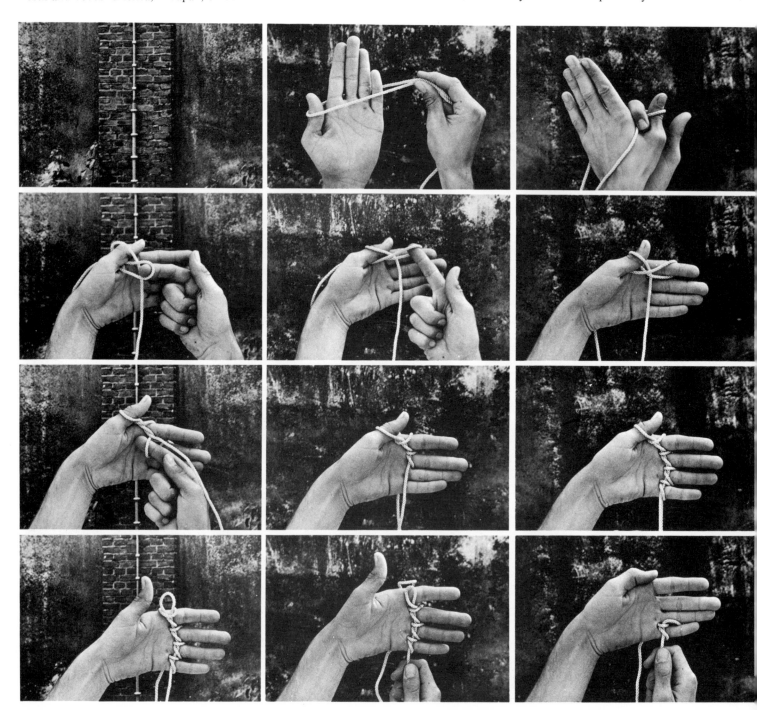

finger of the left hand.

– Put the right index finger, now left of the front line, between the index finger and middle finger, hook the fingertip over the back line, pull it towards you, make another half-turn and lay the loop around the middle finger.

– Do the same around the ring finger and little finger.

– Slide all the loops down the fingers and pull the string taut by the hanging loop.

– Slide the loop off the thumb.

– Pull on the front hanging line and the mouse is gone.

In Germany this trick is known as The Express Train: the loop around the thumb is the locomotive, the loops around the other fingers are first class, second class, buffet car and luggage van. Whistle as you slide the loop off your thumb and the express train disappears as if by magic.

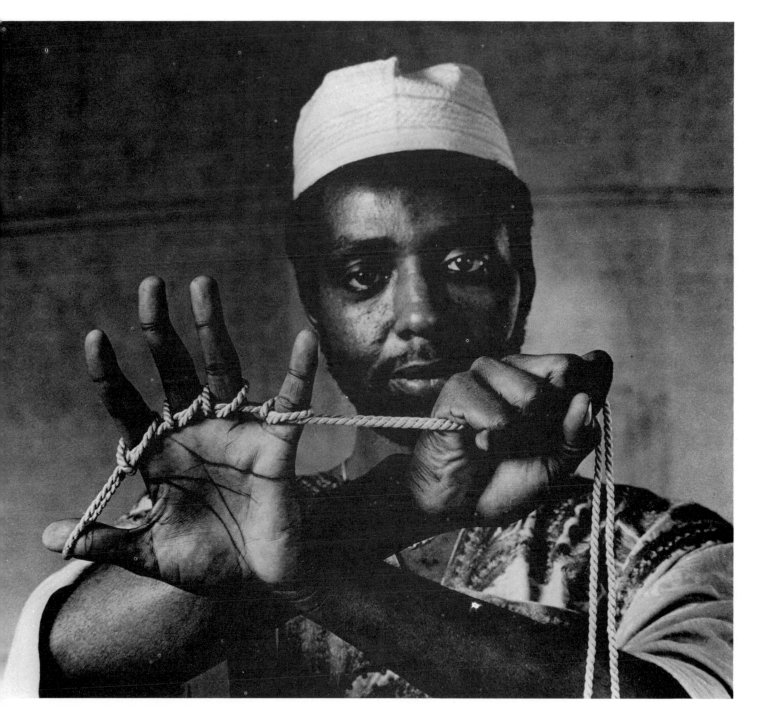

The Smith's Secret 2

This trick is attributed to the Eskimos of Alaska. The secret is in the thumb.
– Take the string circle doubled in the right hand, lay the end around the left little finger and stretch both lines in front of the inside of the fingers.
– Bend the ring finger and take the outer line on the back of it. With the right hand take the twist out of the string.
– In the same way take the outer line on the back of the middle finger and then the index finger (and take the twist out of the string).
– Take the doubled string and lay both lines round the back of the thumb; the line which comes from behind the index finger is underneath.
– Now stretch the two lines in front of the palm of the hand.
– Take the bottom line on the back of the index finger over the top line and take the twist out of the string.
– Repeat this with the middle finger, ring finger and little finger. Pull the double string taut.
– Take the loops off the thumb and pull on both lines with the right hand.

   The Eskimos play this game on two hands at once and with some practice you can do this too. Stretch the string circle over the two little fingers. If both hands do the same thing at the same time the string will not become twisted. Watch that the lines coming from behind the index fingers are on the thumbs under the other lines. Finally, free both thumbs and pull the hands vigorously apart.

The Wigwam

See the photograph on page 48.

The Indian tent that we call a 'wigwam' is called a 'hogan' by the Navaho Indians.

- Hold the string circle double between the index finger and middle finger of the left hand in such a way that there is a loop of about 15 cm hanging down behind the hand, and a long loop hanging down in front of the palm.
- Take the small loop over the index finger and middle finger to the left of the index finger and to the right of the middle finger.
- From the back, put the right hand through the long loop, put the right index finger (above the small loop) under the double line between the index finger and middle finger and pull it out completely, through the large loop. You should now be holding a double long loop in your hand.
- Divide the bottom double line of this loop: lay the right line around the thumb and the left line around the little finger of the left hand.
- Let go of the string with the right hand.
- Take hold of the line running straight across the knot with the thumb and index finger of the right hand and, with the fingertips, pull it up as far as possible above the flat, spread hand.

Two Diamonds

This simple figure originated amongst the Osage Indians. You need a smaller string circle, about 1.5 metres long, or use a larger one doubled up as in pages 50–51.

– Do opening A, free the thumbs.
– Bend the thumbs over the first three lines, under the back line and then pull it towards you.
– Bend the thumbs over the side lines and put them into the index finger loops from below. Pull the string taut.

– Do a Navaho leap over the thumbs.
– From above, put the index fingers into the triangles next to the thumbs, press the fingertips on to the ball of the thumb, turn the palms down and free the little fingers.
– Spread the thumbs and index fingers (see pages 50–51).

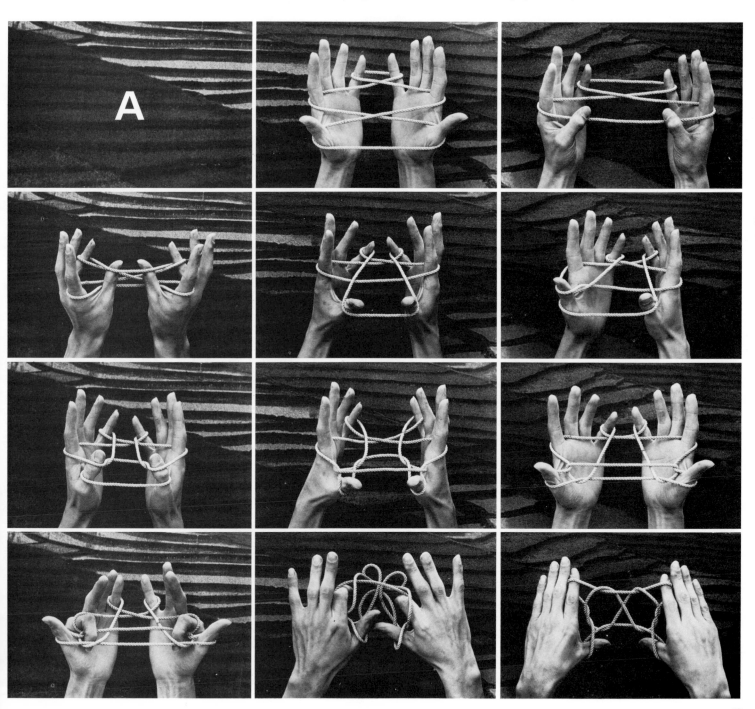

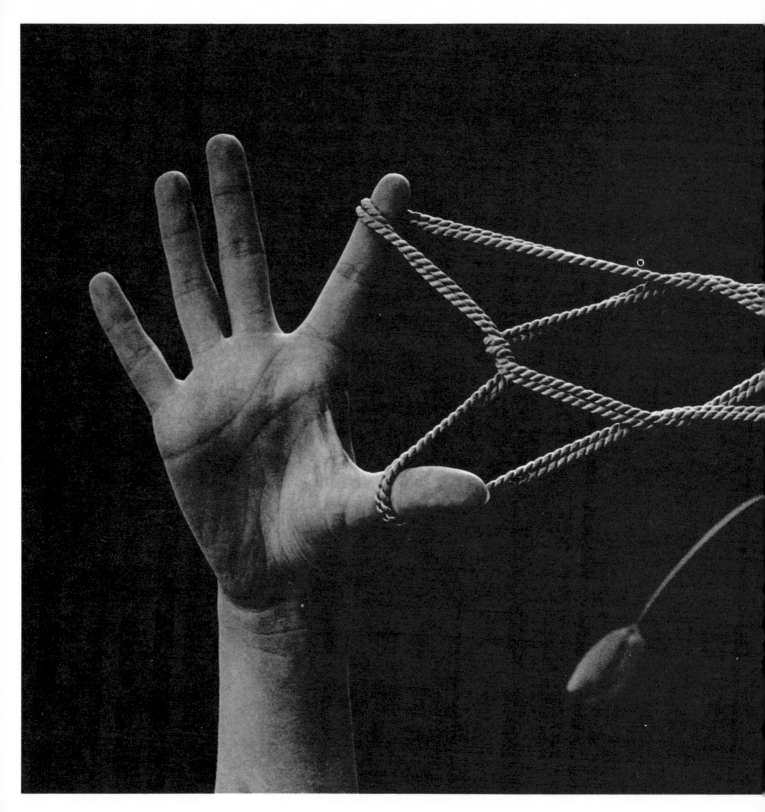

Weaving on a hand-loom

A game to do together: one holds the hands up and the other weaves
The Tortoise (see page 63). It is quite difficult to hold up the string
if you have small hands, so don't take on too much.

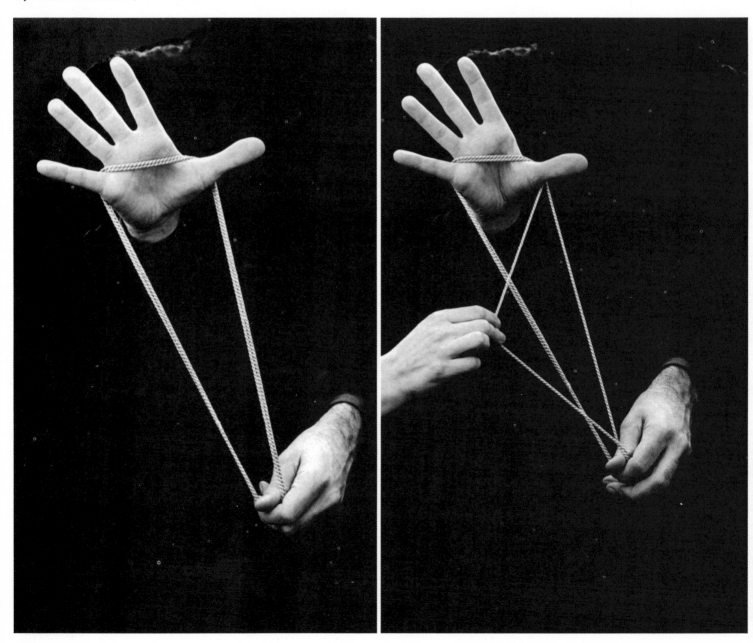

The Hammock

It is possible to make this Indian string figure by yourself (with a doorknob) but you can also do it together.

1 Take the string circle double and put one end round the doorknob and the other round your hand in first position 1 (see page 52).
2 Take one of the front lines, pull it back over all the other lines, pull one of the back lines up, over the first, let the first one drop, take up the third line, take it between the first and second and lay it around the little finger.
3 Pull the diagonal line (by the doorknob) over the front line, take the front line over it, drop the former and lay the other around the thumb.
4 Pull the front line over the second, take the second over it, drop the first, pull the second over it and so on. Lay the last over the little finger.
5 Begin again with the diagonal line and repeat 3 and 4 again and again, as long as you have any string left.
6 Finally, lay the loop of the doorknob over the top of the index finger (see pages 56–7).

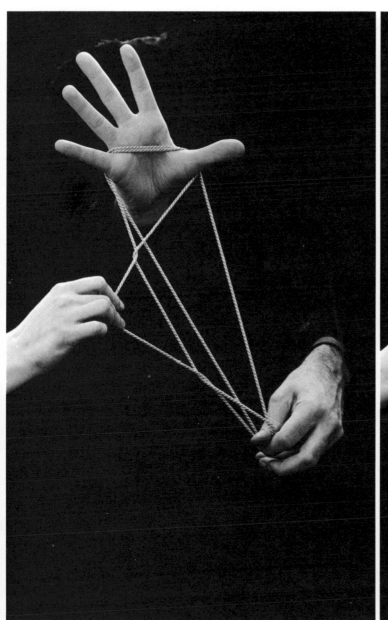
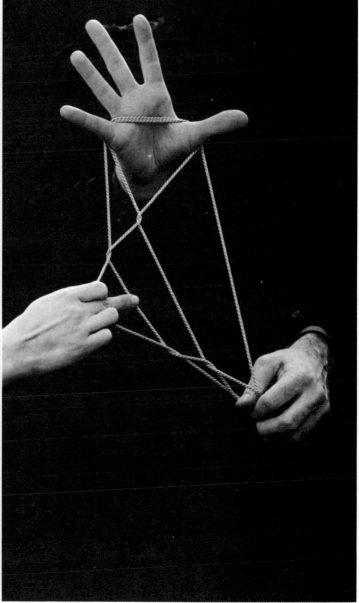

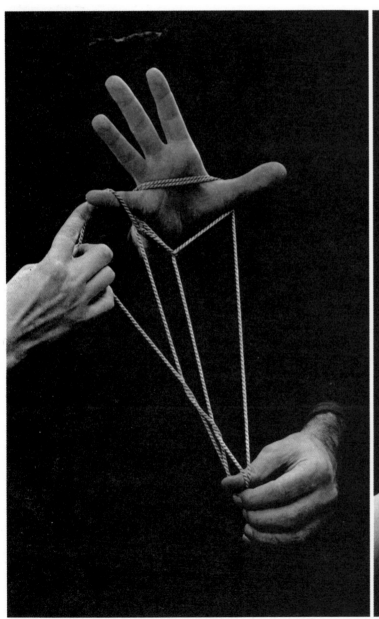 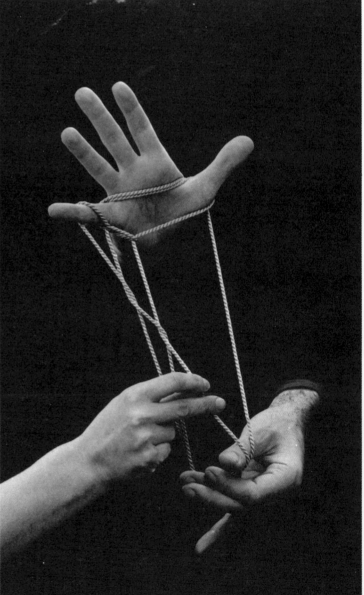

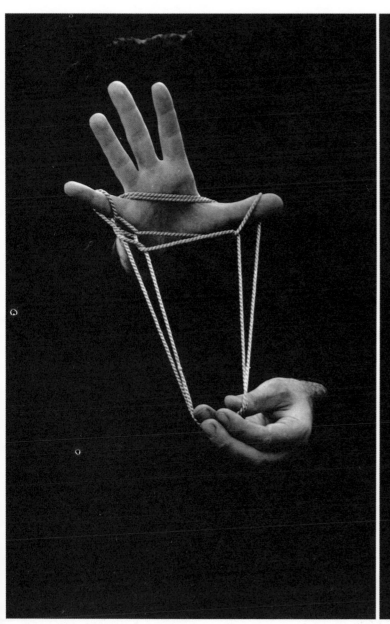
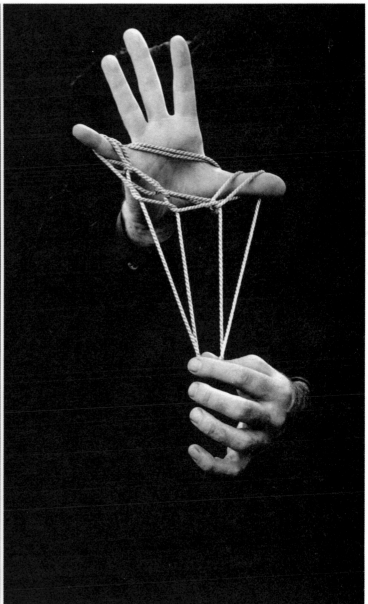

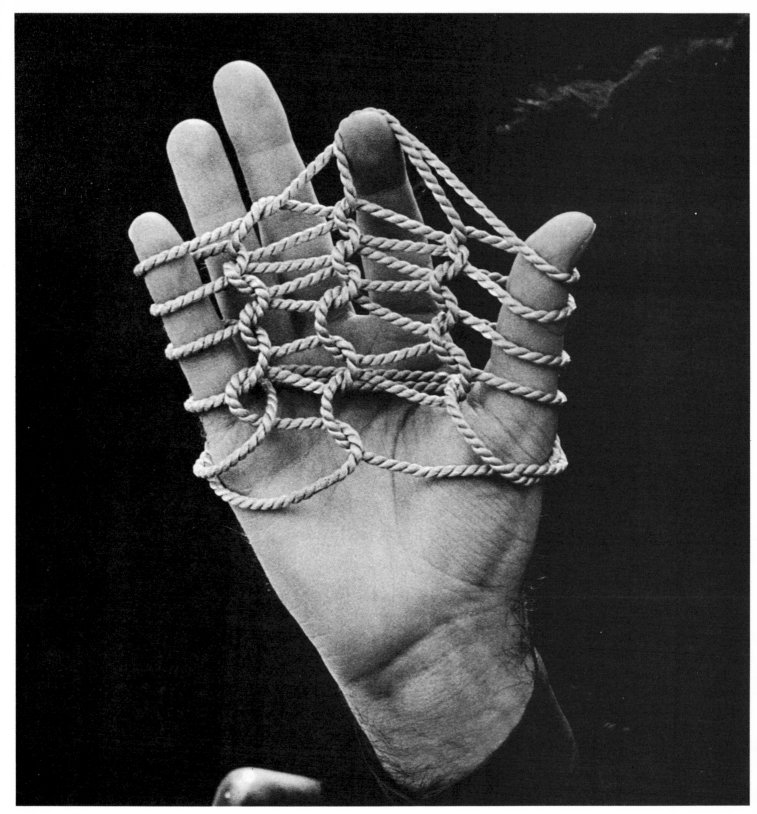

Weaving for two

Use a string circle 3 metres long or longer.

A Do the ribcage opening (see page 26). Pull all the lines taut, the fingers pointing to **B.**

B Pull the bottom line up over the next line (it doesn't matter which of the two), pull this second line through under the first, let go of the first, pull up the second, pull the third underneath, let go of the second, pull the fourth under the third, and so on. Slide the crossovers which are made on the left and right, towards the fingers. When the last line has been pulled under the last but one line, it can be laid over the thumbs. Now go back: pull the top line down, take the second over it and continue down to the bottom line, which can be laid around the little fingers. In this way you can go on weaving as long as there is string between the fingers (see page 62).

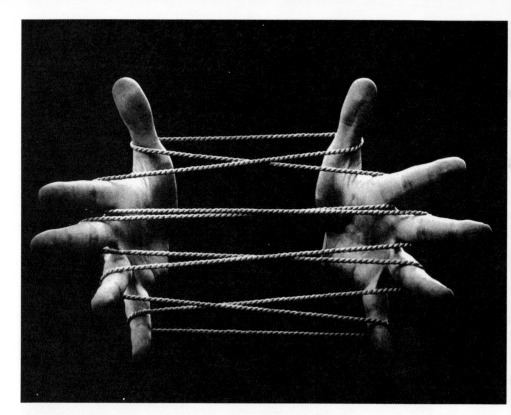

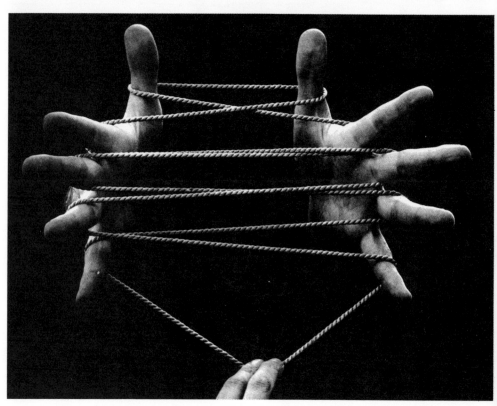

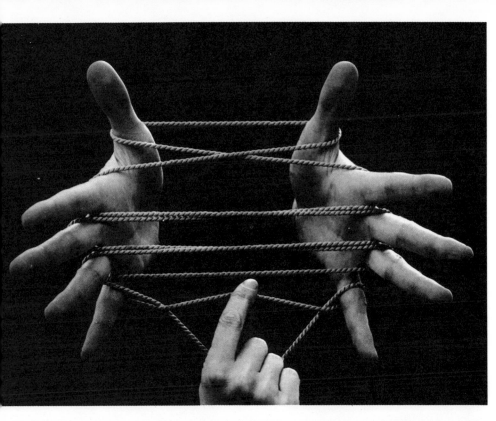

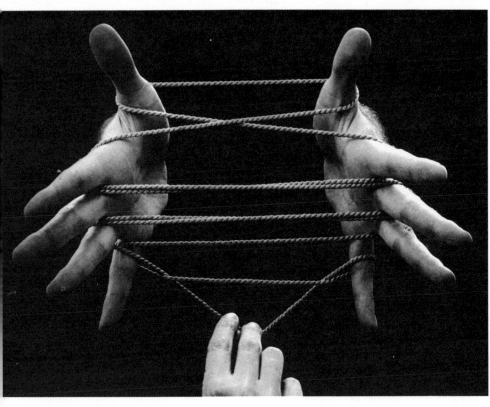

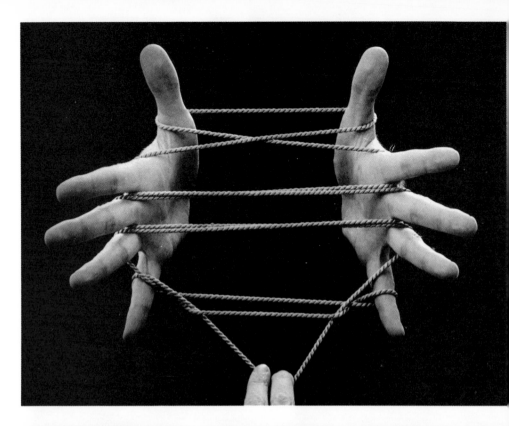

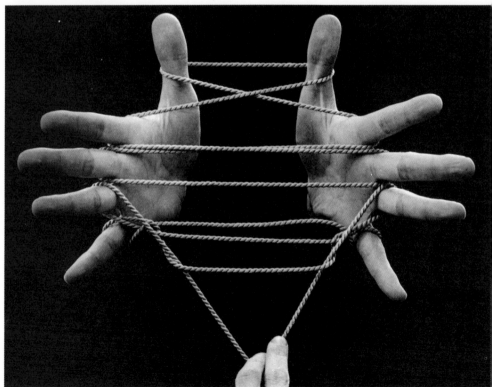

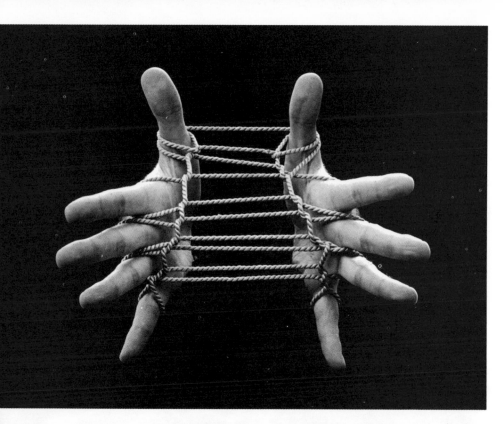

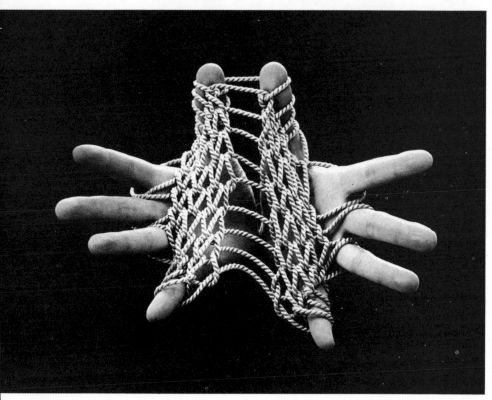

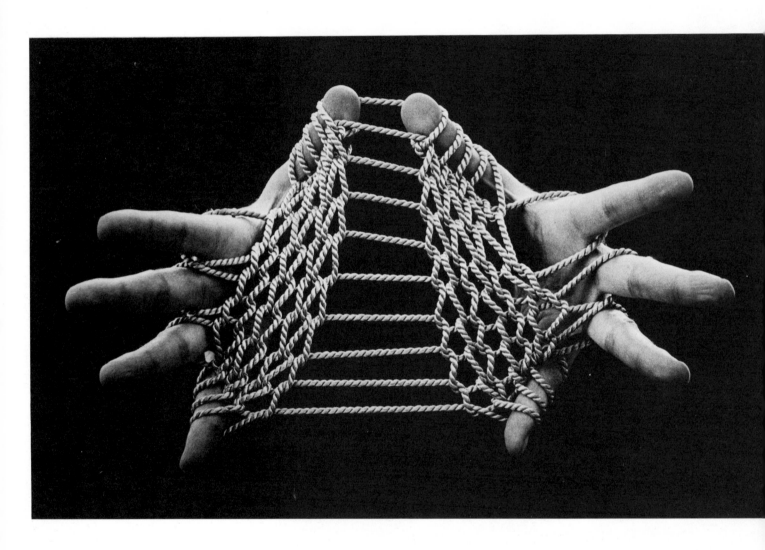

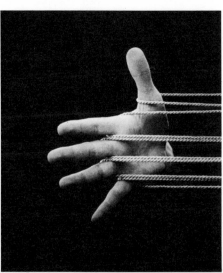

Weaving for four strong hands – The Tortoise

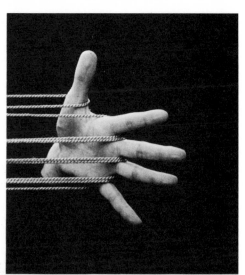

It is possible to weave with one small hand and a string circle, but if you use a rope that is 5 or 6 metres long, you really need four strong hands: both the weaving and holding the rope require strength. Apart from this, however, it is exactly the same as the last figure.

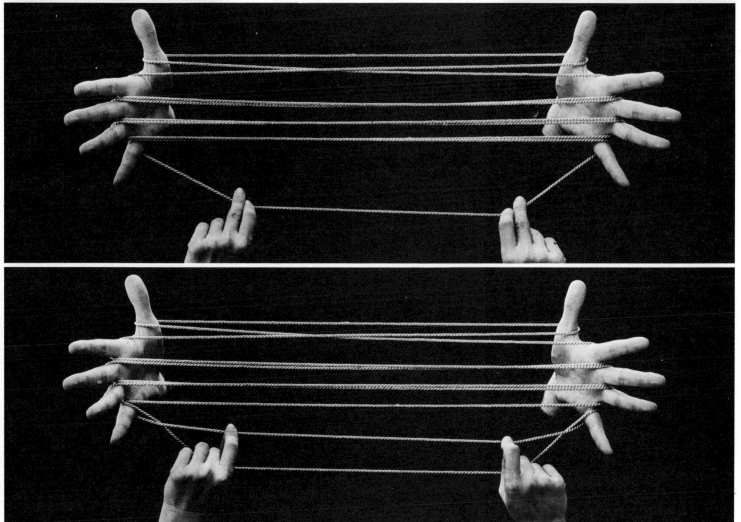

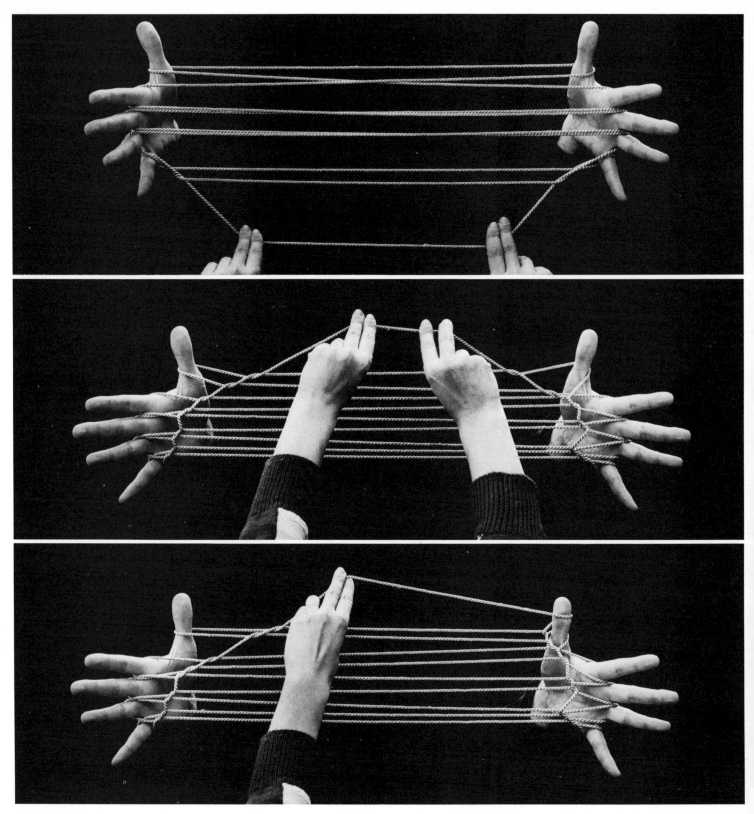

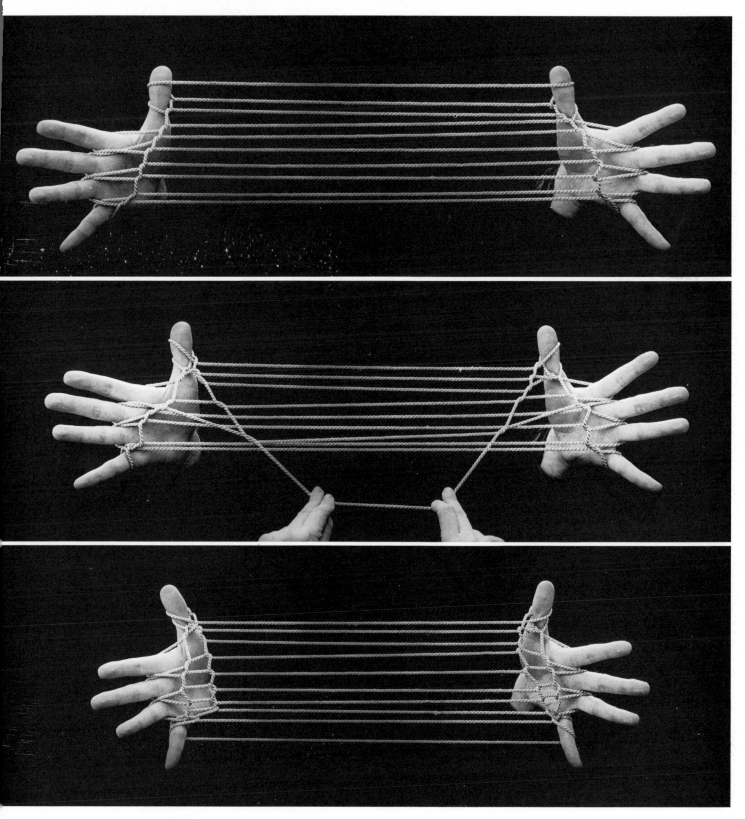

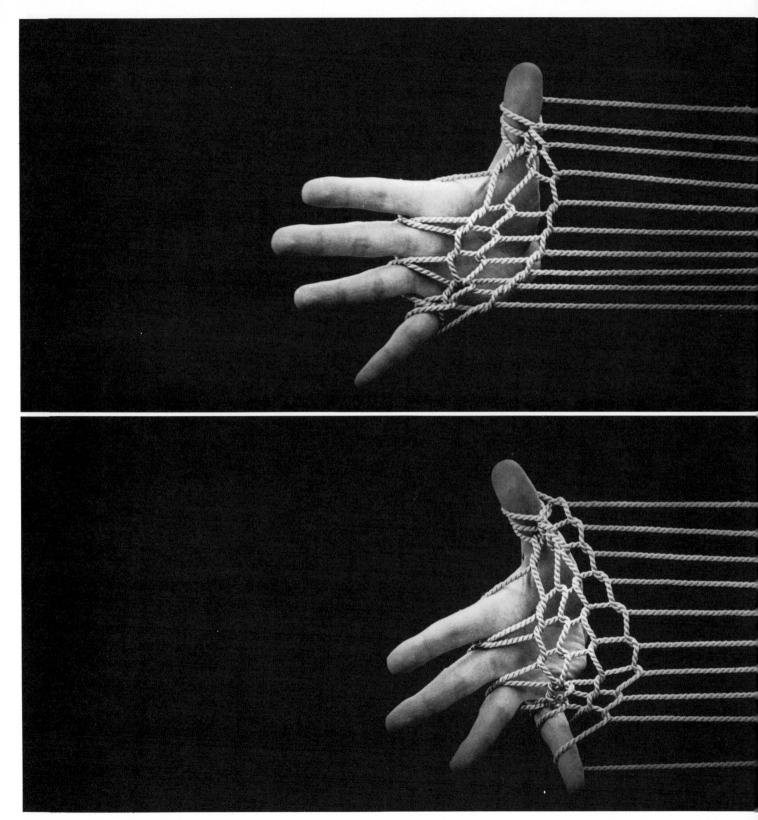

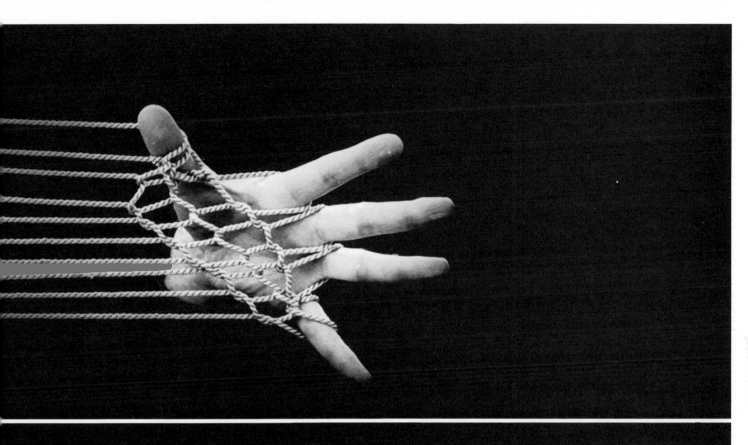

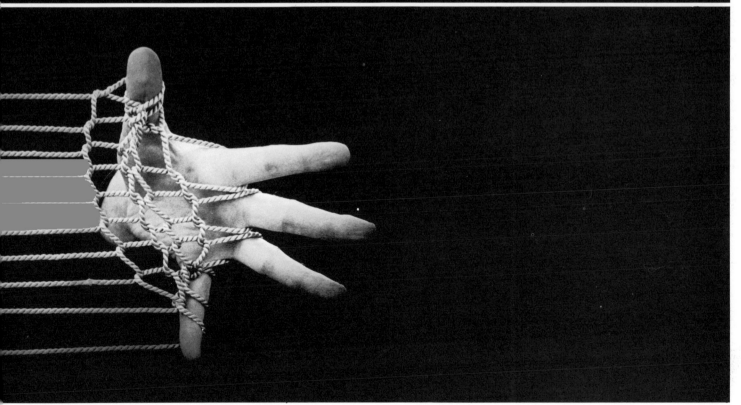

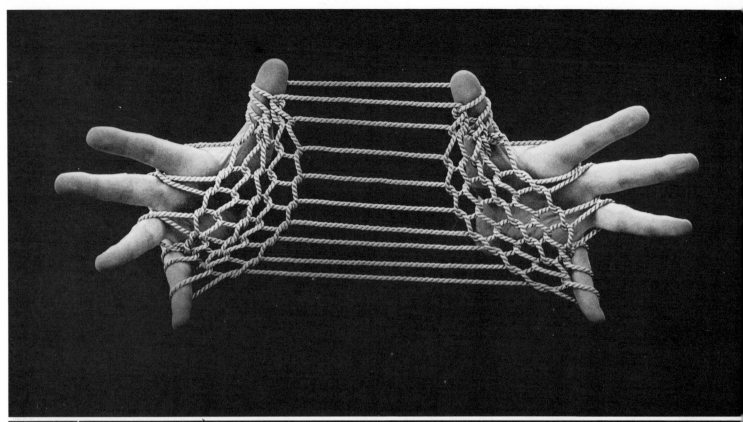

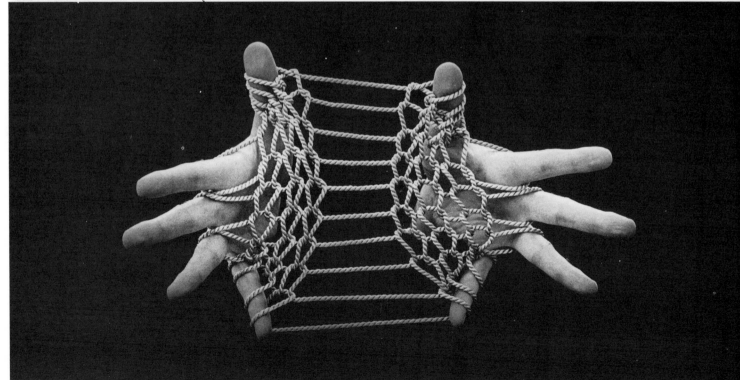

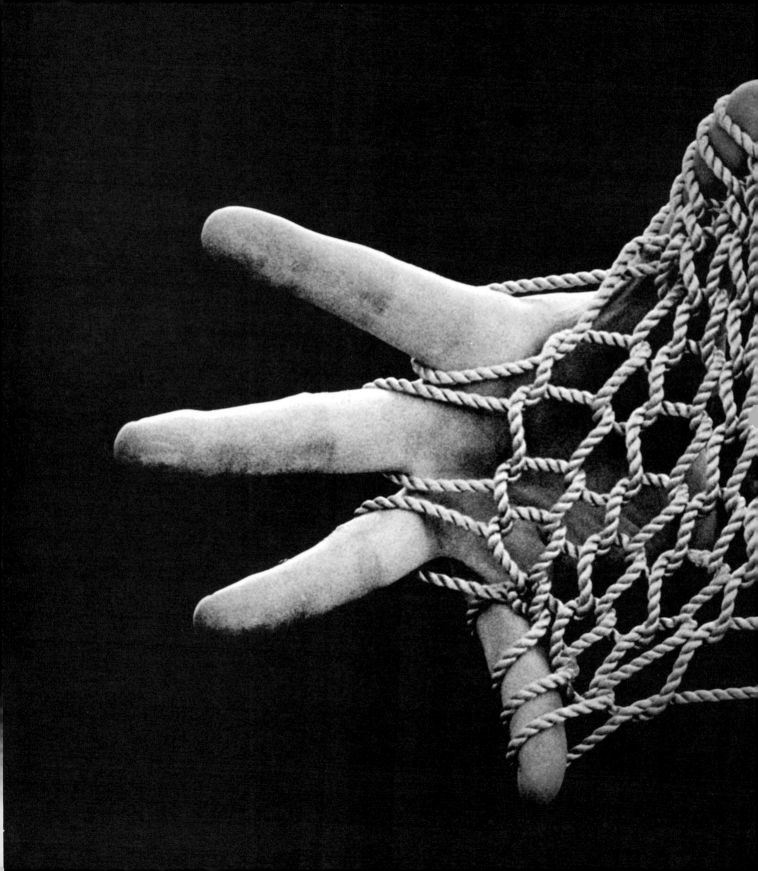

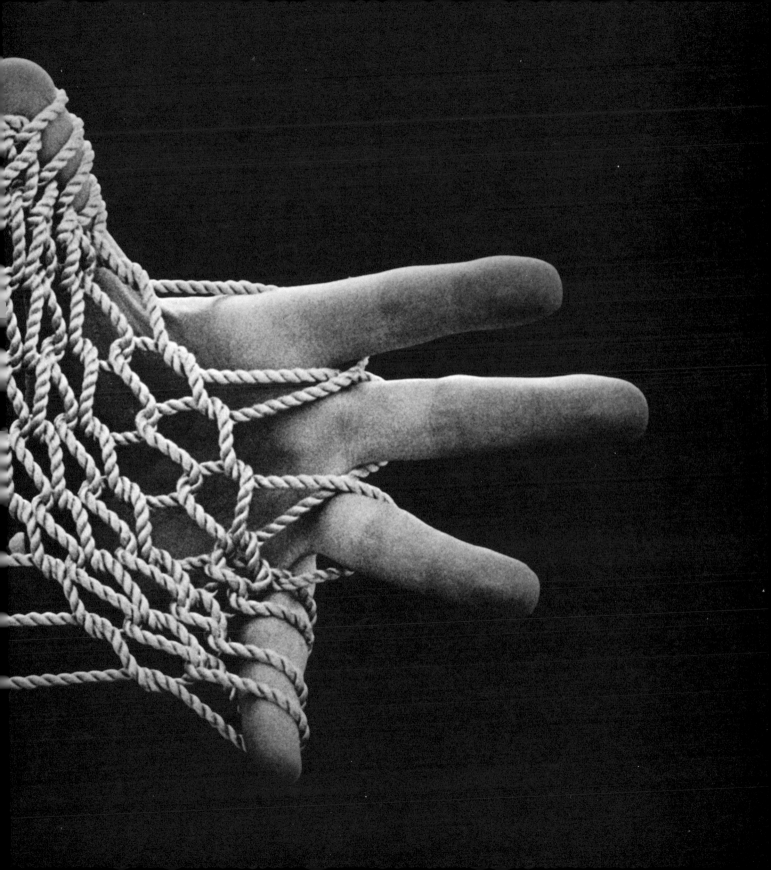

The Ribcage

This figure comes from the Eskimos in Alaska; it looks complicated but is easy to do because there are five Navaho leaps in it.

You need a string circle at least 2 metres long.
– Do the ribcage opening (see page 26).
– From the front, put the thumbs between the crossed lines between thumb and index finger and pull the top lines towards you on the thumbs. Do a Navaho leap on both thumbs.
– Repeat this: thumbs between the crossed lines in front of the middle finger, pull the top lines towards you and do the Navaho leap.
– Do it again: this time between the crossed lines in front of the ring finger, pull them

towards you and do another Navaho leap.
– Now take care – in front of the little fingers the lines are the other way round. The lines which are to go on the thumbs come from behind the little fingers and should be pulled over the others. Then do a Navaho leap.

– Pull the line behind the little fingers towards you on the thumbs. Do a Navaho leap.
– From above, take the thumb loops on to the little fingers and pull the front line towards you with the thumbs or teeth (see page 74).

The Flying Bird

This suggestive figure originates in the South Sea Islands.

– Hang the string circle around your neck.
– Do position 1 with the hanging loop (see page 22).
– Do opening A (see page 24).
– From the front, put the thumbs between the crossed lines in front of the index fingers; pull the top lines towards you on the thumbs and do a Navaho leap under the neck loop.
– From above, put the little fingers between the crossed lines linking the little fingers and index fingers and pull the front two lines back with the little fingers.
– Do a Navaho leap over the two little fingers.
– Let the string slide off the index fingers.
– Move the hands up and down, moving the little fingers and thumbs apart and together again rhythmically and you will see a flying bird.

The Gated Well

Another extremely visual figure originating from the South Sea Islands.
– Do opening A (see page 24).
– Move the index fingers over the back crossed lines, pull these two lines towards you with bent index fingers and stretch out the index fingers again between the front crossed lines.
– Free the little fingers.
– From above, put the free fingers of both hands in the index finger loops and press the back double lines against the palms.

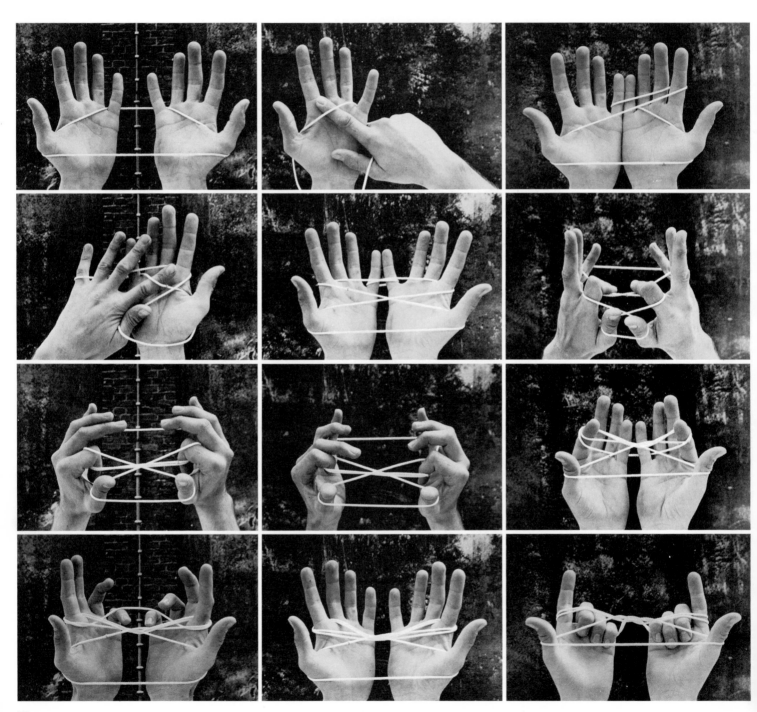

– Carefully free the left thumb, put this thumb over the line which has just been released on the left behind the diagonal line between the index finger and the bottom of the figure, and take this line on the thumb. Do the same on the right and make the well by spreading the tops of the thumbs and index fingers.

– Put the thumbs of both hands behind the double line just in front of the index fingers.

– Do a Navaho leap with the thumb loops.

– Take all of the fingers out of the loops, except for the thumbs, and let the figure hang.

– From behind, put all the free fingers into the thumb loops and make the figure by spreading the hands: The Gated Well.

The Spectacles

This figure was invented by the Zulus and is also known as The Moth. You need a shorter string circle than usual (or use a long one doubled up).

– Do opening A (see page 24).
– Free the thumbs.
– From above, put the thumbs on both sides of the crossover between the crossed lines and pull the front little finger lines towards you on the thumbs.
– Free the little fingers.
– From below, put both thumbs into the index finger loops.
– Do a Navaho leap over the two thumbs (see page 30).
– Put both index fingers in the triangles next to the thumbs, move the palms downwards – the original index finger loops slide off – and spread the thumbs and index fingers.

Man in a Hammock

– Place the string circle over your wrists.
– With the right hand take the double line (by the left hand), lay the front line between the thumb and index finger, the back line between the middle finger and ring finger,

and pull both back between the index finger and middle finger.
– Lay the front line behind the thumb, the back line around the little finger.
– From below, put the right index finger and middle finger in the corresponding loops of the left hand, and do a Navaho leap over the left hand.

– Slide the loops of the right index finger and middle finger over the corresponding fingers on the left.
– Do a Navaho leap over the left index finger and middle finger.
– Take the loops of those fingers over to the corresponding fingers on the right (see pages 82–3).

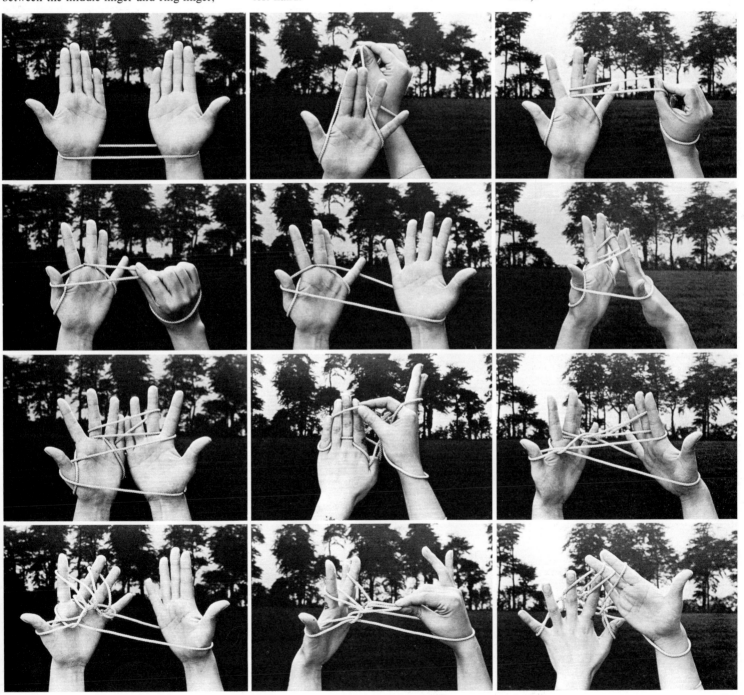

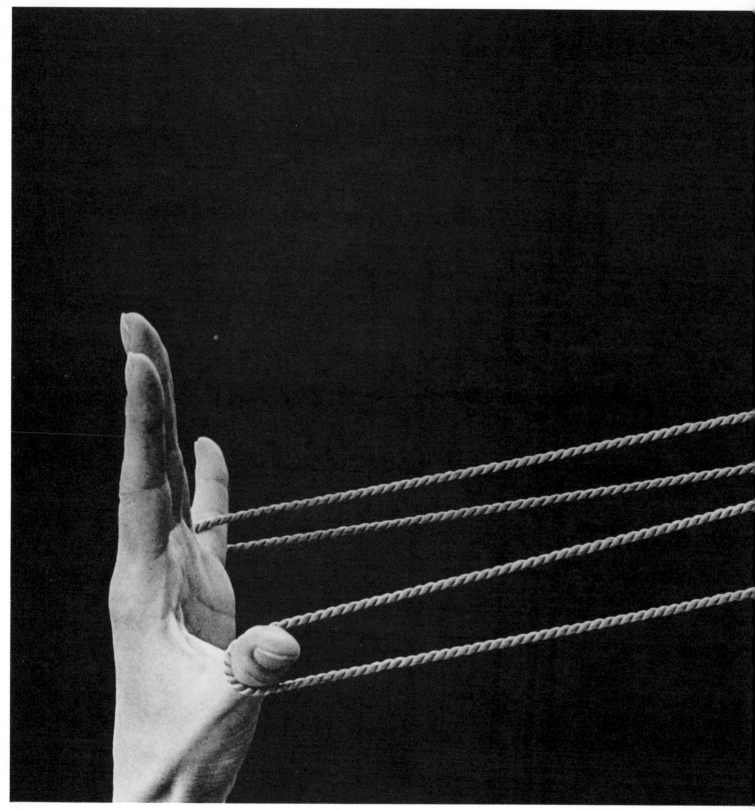

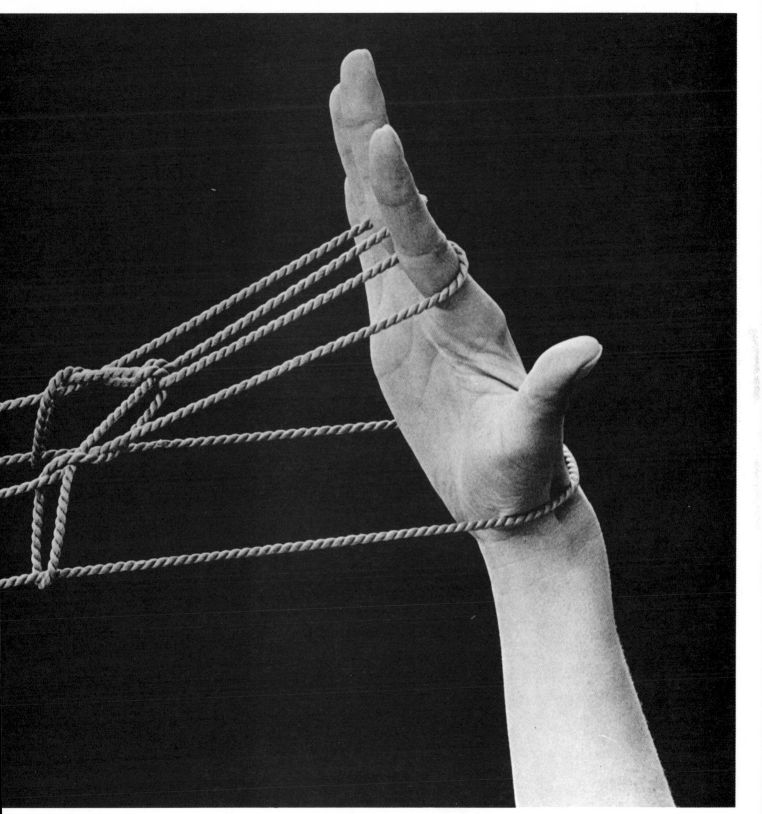

The Butterfly

This figure was first found amongst the Navaho Indians. It has also been found in other places and is sometimes known as The Snail because it crawls slowly forward.
– Do the Navaho opening (see page 28).
– Hold the thumb lines securely so that they cannot slip away. Turn the index finger lines fives times with the fingertips.
– From below, put the thumbs into the index finger loops and do a Navaho leap (see page 30) with the thumb lines over both thumbs.
– Press the tops of the thumbs together, press the index fingertips together and let the loops slide from the right hand to the left hand

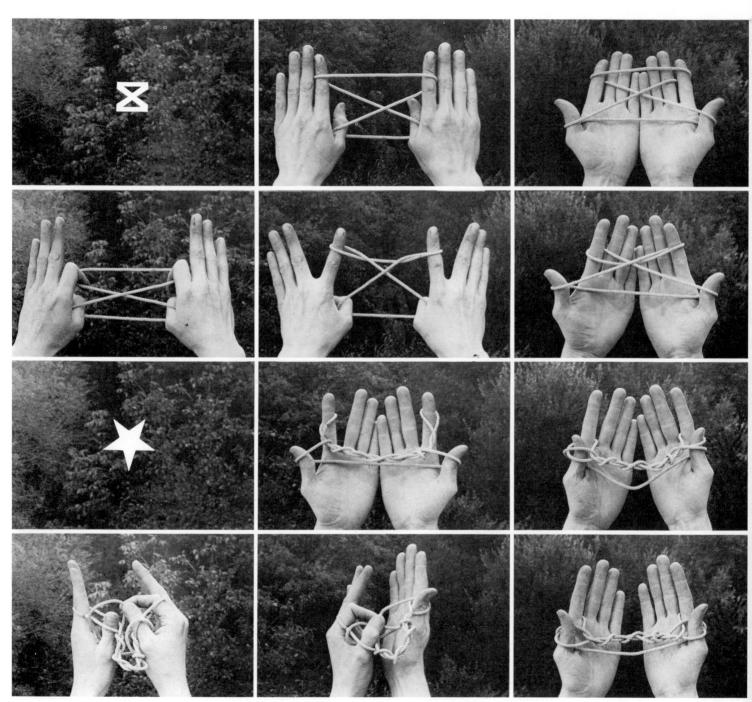

– From the front, hook the right thumb and index finger under the left thumb, between the two hanging thumb loops. Take the left loop on to the thumb, the right loop on to the index finger of the right hand.
– Take the two loops from the left index finger with the right thumb and index finger, put the left thumb and index finger between the two loops and take the back loop on the index finger and the front loop on the thumb of the left hand.
– Move the hands apart a little and the middle lines roll up. From above, put the free fingers of both hands into the index finger loops and from below into the thumb loops and pull them down. By moving the hands slightly the butterfly flutters or the snail crawls forward (see page 86).

Man in Bed

As they played this string game, little Indian children would sing a song which showed that the man in bed, a paleface, was certainly not very popular with them:

'Man in bed, man in bed, lying there fast asleep,
Lying there fast asleep, the bed breaks.'

– Do opening A (see page 24).
– Slide the lines on the index fingers up a little, bend the thumbs under them, and from below pull the front little finger lines towards you.

– From above, put the little fingers into the index finger loops, under the back thumb lines and pull them back through the index finger loops.
– Now free the index fingers. The paleface is lying in bed (below left). As you say 'breaks', free the little fingers and the bed collapses (below right).

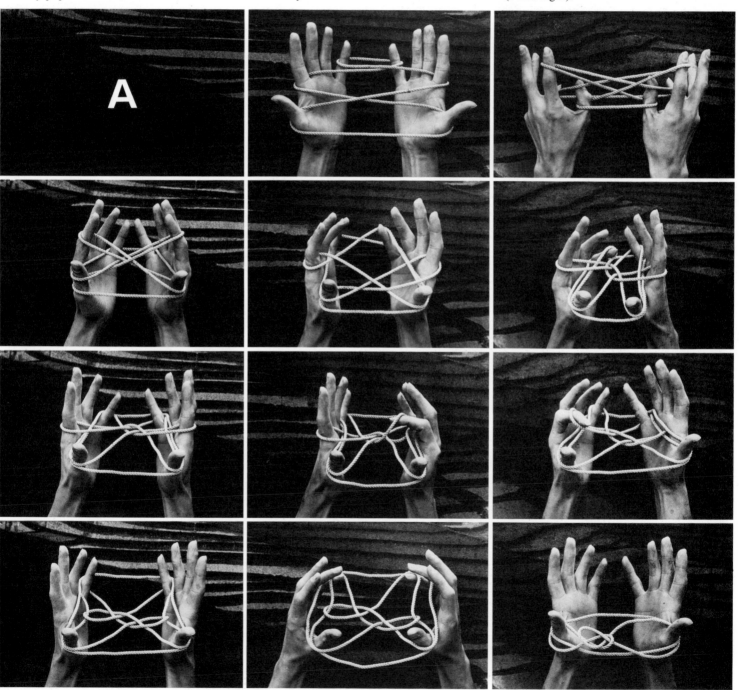

The Apache Door

This string figure is well-known amongst many Indian tribes in North and South America. Every tribe knows it by a different name: The Tent Door, String Bag, Horde, Poncho, Streamers, Fish-Net, and many others. In Europe it is commonly known as The Apache Door.

– Do opening A (see page 24).
– Take the string from the left index finger and lay it over the whole hand around the left wrist. Do the same on the right.
– From below, put the thumbs into the little finger loops and pull the front little finger lines towards you.
– From below, put the little fingers into the thumb loops and pull the back thumb lines back.
– Slide the two lines on the left thumb up, bend the left hand forward with the thumbs spread out, go under all the lines with the thumb and stretch out the thumb and hand

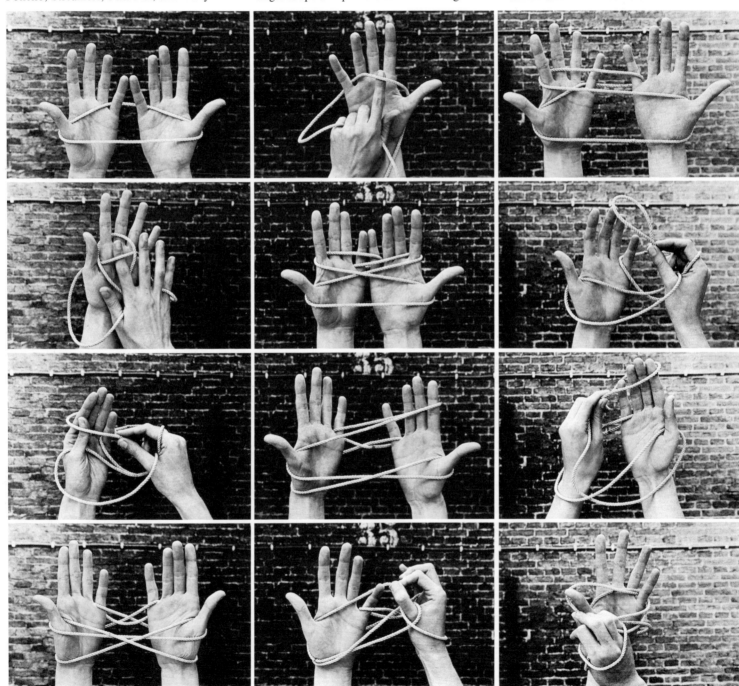

88

again. Take the two loops off the left thumb with the thumb and index finger of the right hand, take the thumb back and put it back in the loops, over all the lines. Do the same on the right.

– On both hands do a Navaho leap over the whole hand with the line behind the wrist.

– Pull the figure taut (see pages 90–92).

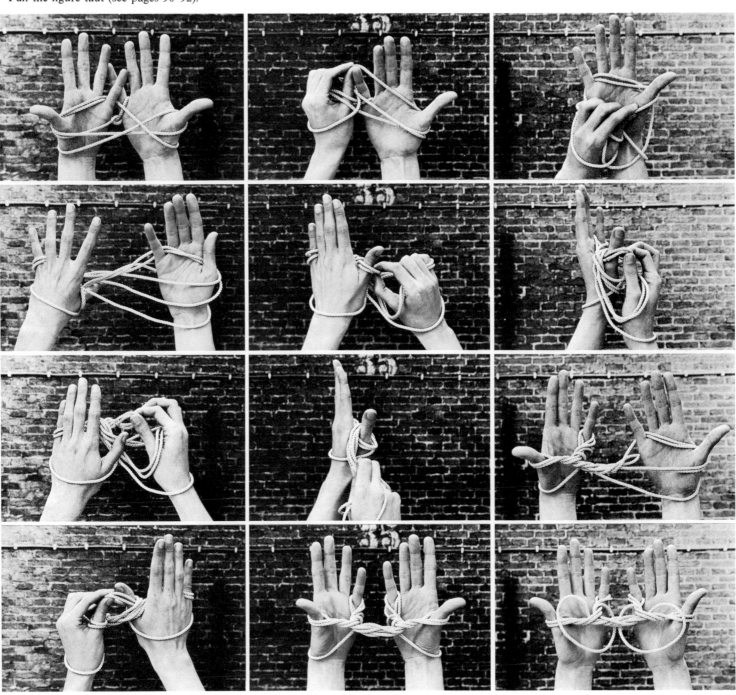

Girl with the Apache Door.

The Kiwi

This bird figure, a sort of ostrich, originates amongst the Maoris of New Zealand.

– Do opening A and free the thumbs.
– Put the thumbs over the front line, under the crossed lines and pull the front little finger line towards you.
– Free the little fingers.
– Bend the little fingers into the index finger loops towards you, under the back thumb lines and pull them back.
– Free the thumbs.

– From above, put the thumbs into the index finger loops under the front little finger lines and pull them towards you.
– Put the index fingers under the front index finger line (holding all the lines securely) and do the Pindiki stroke (see page 28). Then stretch out the kiwi's wings (see pages 94–5).

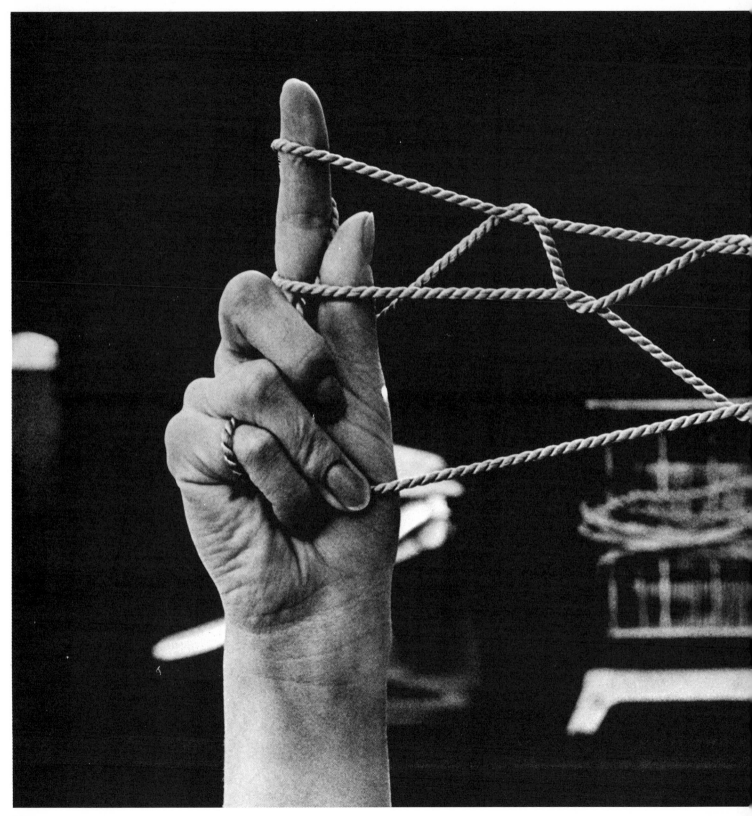

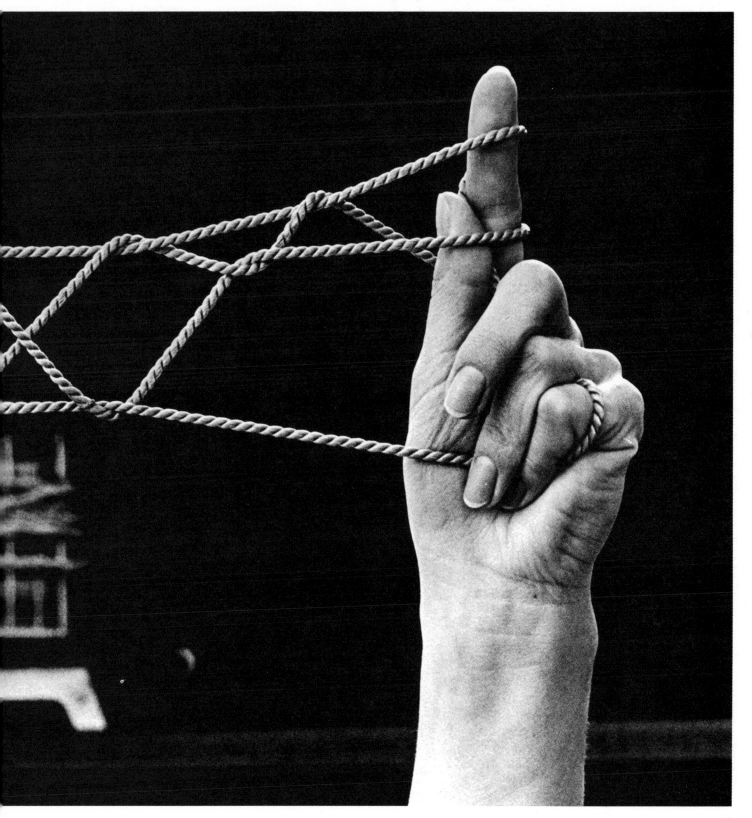

Devika with an imaginative fairy-tale face.

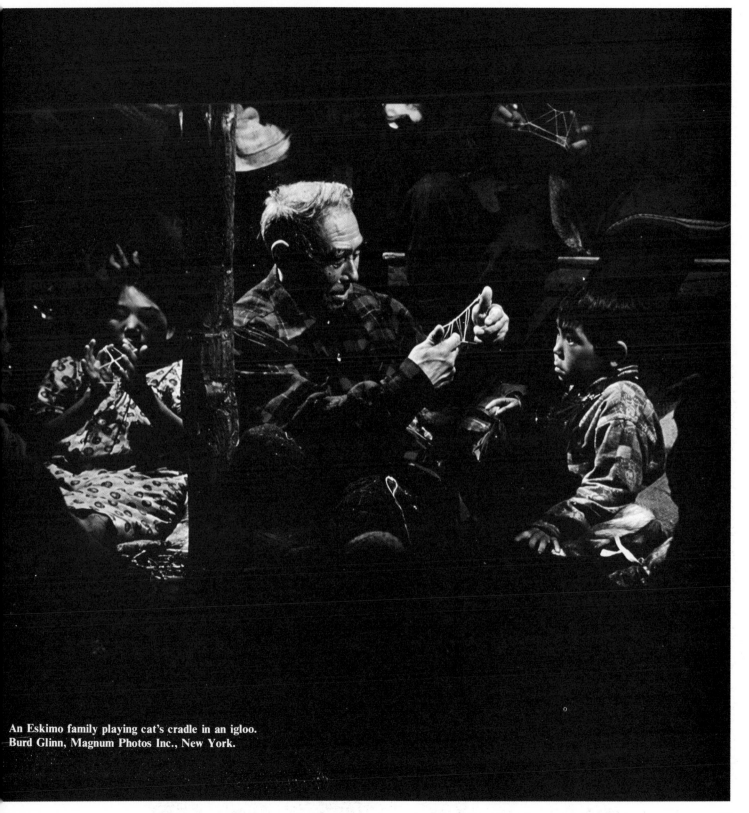

An Eskimo family playing cat's cradle in an igloo.
Burd Glinn, Magnum Photos Inc., New York.

Two women playing *aja-tori* (cat's cradle).
A Japanese woodcut by Haru Nobu, circa 1770.
National Museum, Tokyo.

Illustration from Alice B. Gomme's
'Traditional Games', Part I, Dictionary of
British Folklore, London, 1894.

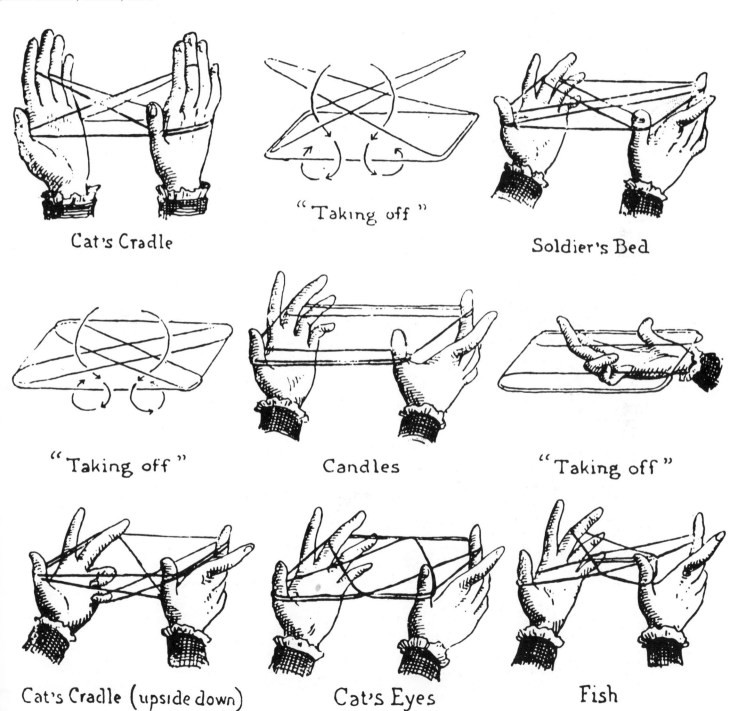

Cat's Cradle

"Taking off"

Soldier's Bed

"Taking off"

Candles

"Taking off"

Cat's Cradle (upside down)

Cat's Eyes

Fish

Cat's Cradle

By far the oldest string game in the world is Cat's Cradle played with two people. Once you've got the feel of it, you can go on endlessly, continually discovering new figures and trying out variations on the familiar patterns. The example shown here gives some idea of the many possibilities.

A does the opening (see page 27); this is The Cradle.

B takes hold of the crossover between finger and thumb from the side, pulls them out and down, under the straight lines and up again with the thumb and index finger stretched up straight. As she puts them up she also takes the straight lines on the thumb and index

The Cradle

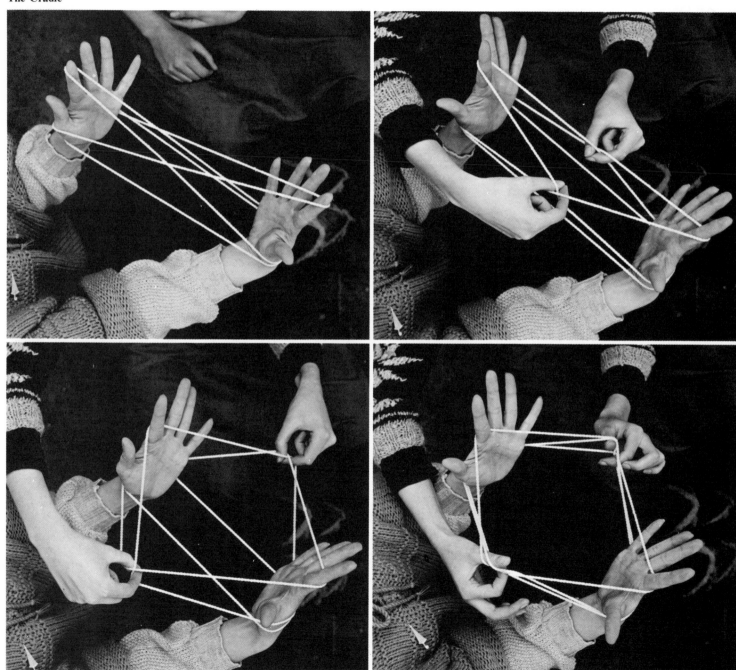

finger. **A** lets go of the string and **B** spreads the thumbs and index fingers. This is The Mattress.

    A takes hold of the crossover of the long lines from above with the finger and thumb and pulls them down to the side under the long lines and up with the thumb and index finger stretched out. She takes the long lines on the thumb and index finger. **B** lets go of the string and **A** spreads the thumbs and index fingers.

The Mattress

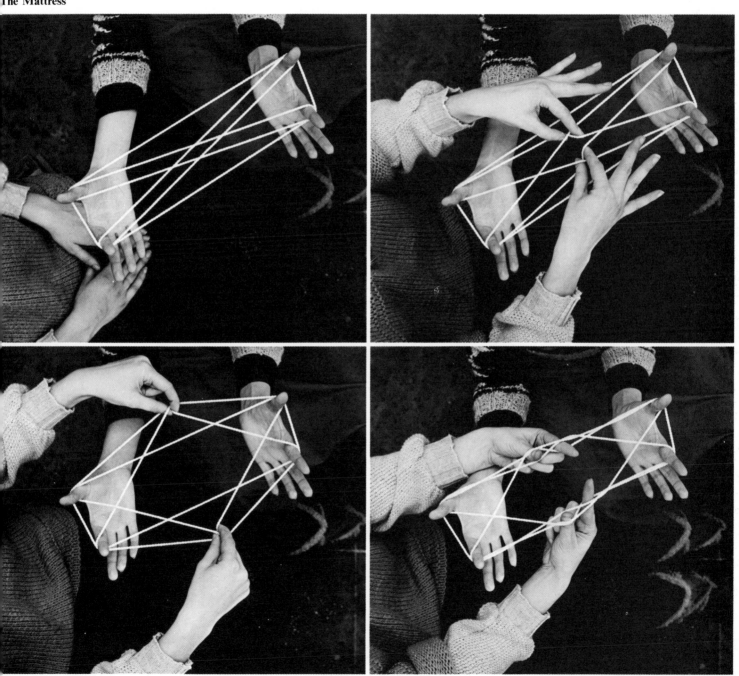

This is The Calm Sea.

 B pulls the single line on the left to the right with the (bent) right little finger, and the single line on the right to the left with the left little finger. Then she puts her hands down, under the double lines and brings them up with the thumb and index finger stretched up. **A** lets go of the string and **B** spreads the thumbs and index fingers.

The Calm Sea

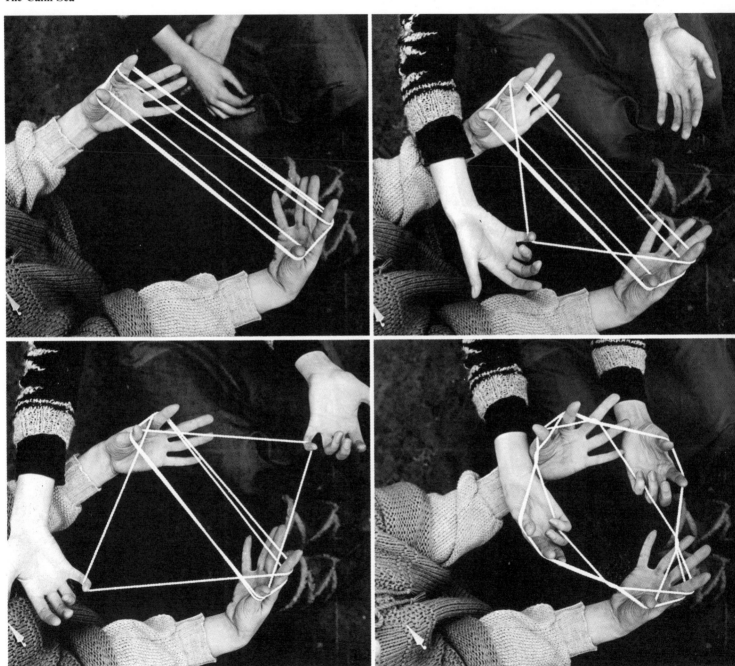

This is The Upturned Cradle.

A takes hold of the crossovers from the side with the finger and thumb, pulls them out and up, over the long straight lines and down. In taking them down she takes the long lines from above with the thumb and index finger. **B** lets go of the string and **A** spreads the thumbs and index fingers.

The Upturned Cradle

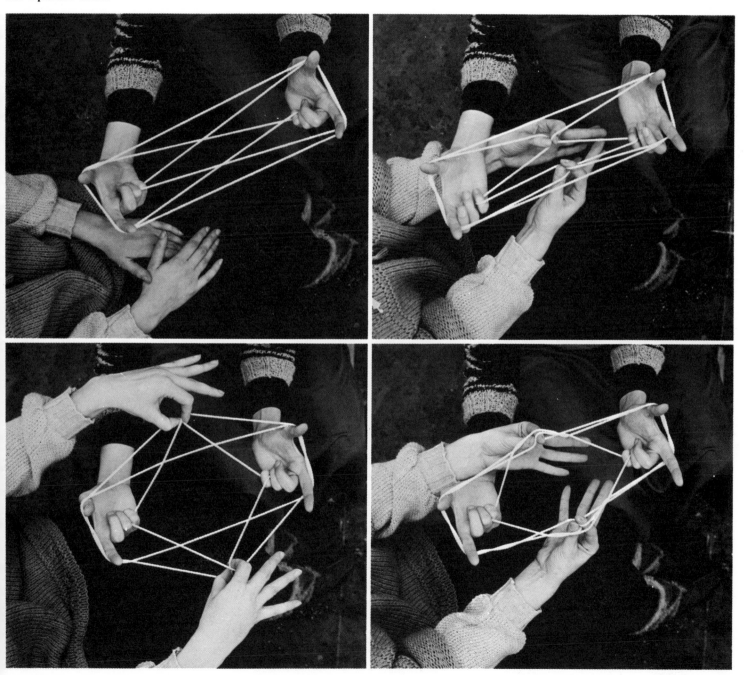

This is The Mattress Turned over.

B pulls the crossovers of the long lines to the side and down from above, under the long lines and up again with thumb and index finger stretched out, taking up the long lines. **A** lets go, **B** spreads thumbs and index fingers.

The Mattress Turned Over (below left)

This is The Cat's Eye.

A takes hold of the crossovers of the diagonal and the long lines and pulls them outwards. **B** lets go.

B takes hold of the crossovers from above, and takes them under the long lines which she takes on to her straightened thumb and index finger. **A** lets go.

A takes hold of the crossovers of the diagonal and long lines from above, turns the thumb and index finger in and up, and pulls the string out.

B lets go and **A** stretches out the (skinned) Pig on the Pegs.

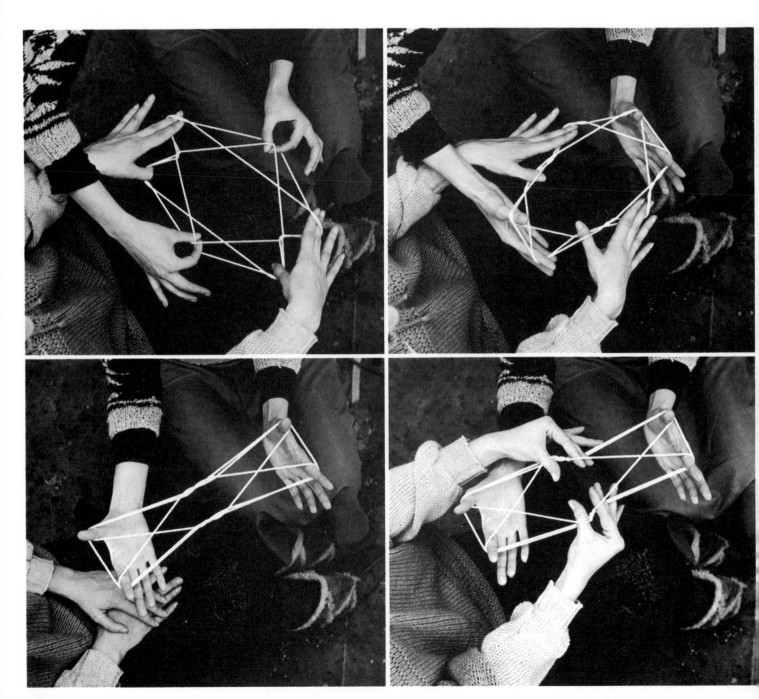

Pig on the Pegs

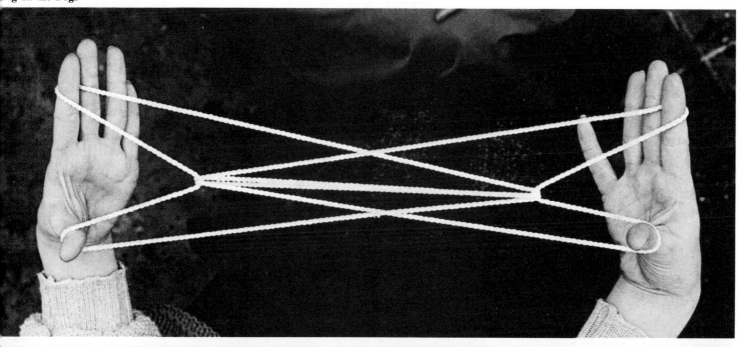

Maori girls playing cat's cradle.
Alexander Turnbull Library, Wellington,
New Zealand.
Photograph from Pieter van Delft's collection.

Shihab (right) playing cat's cradle with the
cook of his Moroccan restaurant in
Amsterdam.

Figures for more than one person

Performance of Sylvia Whitman's Dance Group,
New York, 1975.
Every dancer represents one finger.
Photograph by Babette Mangolte.

The House

An Australian figure for two strings.
It is interesting to try and build this figure from the example shown in the photographs.

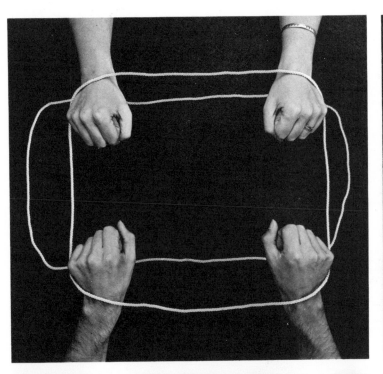

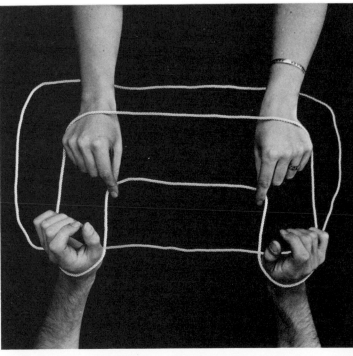

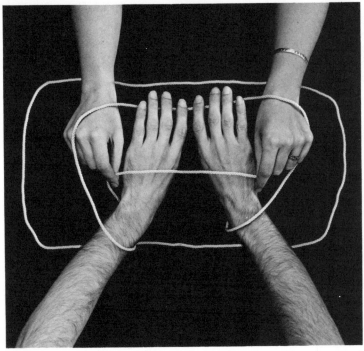

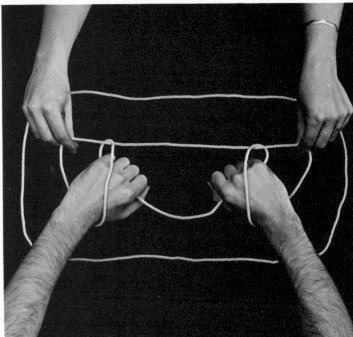

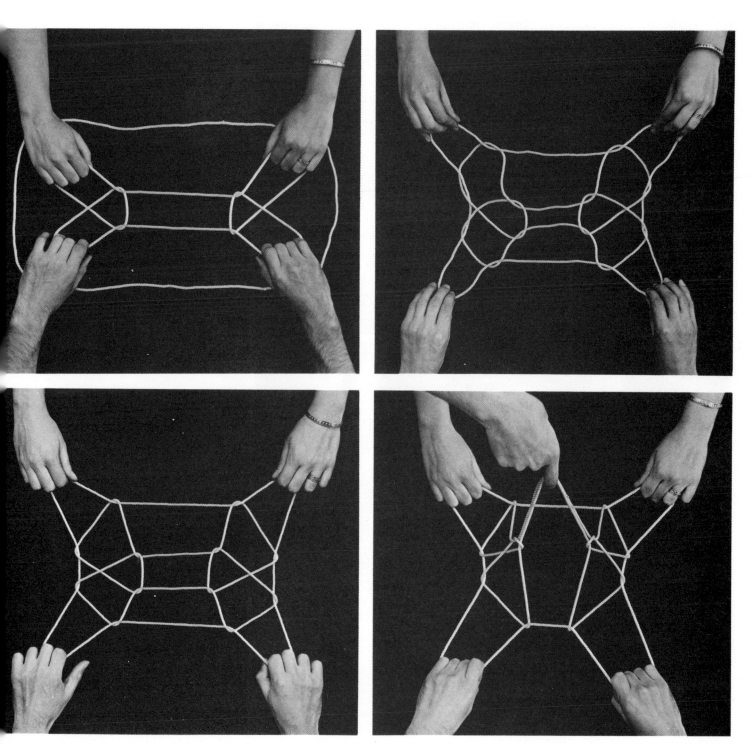

Sawing Together

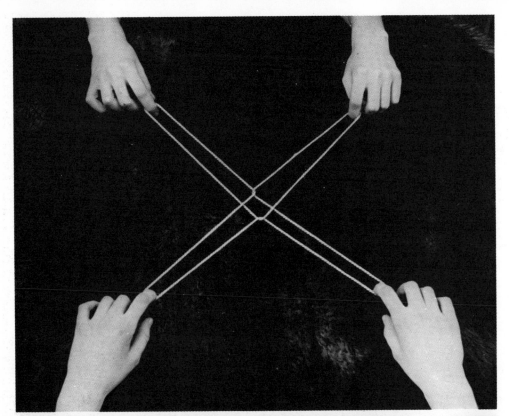

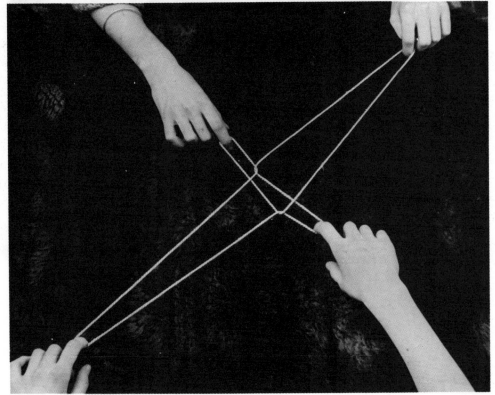

For two people

A game that is played throughout the world.

A does first position 1.

B does first position 1 (from the side with the long lines) and continues with opening A.

A also finishes opening A over B's lines.

A and B free both thumbs and little fingers and pull the string from the side in turn.

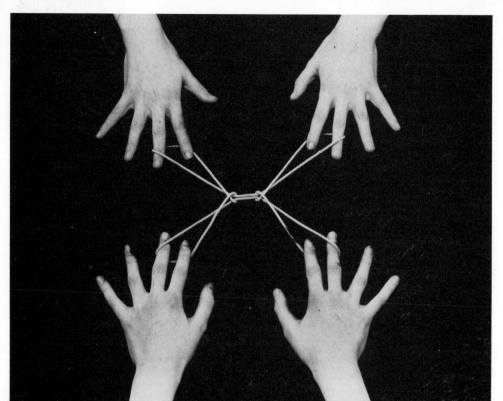

The Stickleback

For two people

This is a string figure from the Guianas that is fun to make with two or more string circles.

A lays down the string circle double between the index fingers and middle fingers of both hands, small loop at the back and the long lines between the hands. Take the small loops to the front: the front lines in front of the index fingers, back lines between the middle fingers and ring fingers. Pull the lines taut. From above, put the index and middle fingers of the left hand behind the loop in front of the index and middle fingers of the right hand, and slide the loops from these fingers on to the corresponding fingers of the left hand.

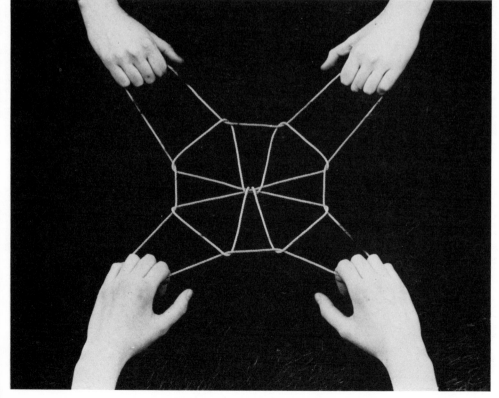

From above, put the index and middle fingers of the right hand at the back of the left hand behind the bottom loops of the corresponding fingers of the left hand. Pass these loops on to the right index and middle fingers. Pull the lines taut. Slide the crossovers of the lines to the centre, take the loops off the fingers and lay the whole thing down flat.

A and **B** put each hand through a loop and pull the second string circle through it, and stretch the whole figure, pulling one outside line out. Now it is possible to make all sorts of figures by sliding, pulling or lifting the string circles or by adding other string circles (see photographs).

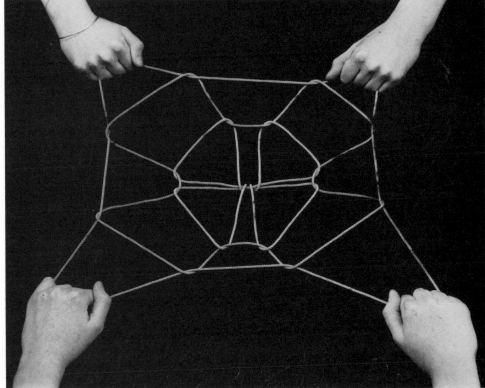

The Star of David and The Hut

For two people

The Pueblo Indians call this figure *Nathu* which means 'hut'.

A does first position 2.
– From above, put the right index finger behind the short diagonal line across the left hand, do half a turn clockwise and pull the lines tight. From below, put the right thumb into the top index finger loop and widen it.
– Now do the same on the left hand, turning it half-way in an anti-clockwise direction (stay between the thumb and index finger loops).
– With the right hand close to the left hand take up all the lines on the left hand, carefully move them off the fingers, do half a turn clockwise and then put them back with the thumb and index finger loops changed round. Do the same with the right hand making half a turn in an anti-clockwise direction.

B takes hold of the crossover in the middle with finger and thumb and pulls it up: you will see a hut made of sticks.

A presses the tops of the thumbs and index fingers of both hands together, bends the hands inwards and spreads the thumbs and index fingers with the palms of the hands facing down.

B hooks with the little fingers the middle part of the front and back parallel lines to the front and back respectively. Let go of the crossover and pull the little fingers further out.

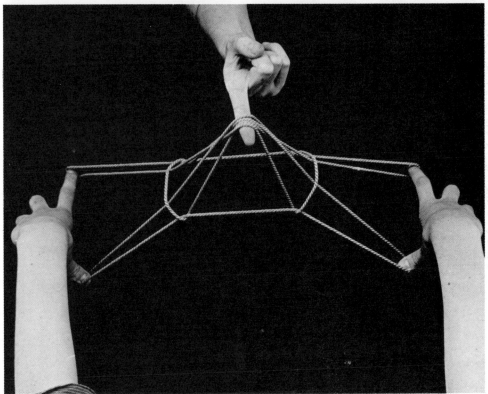

The Hawk

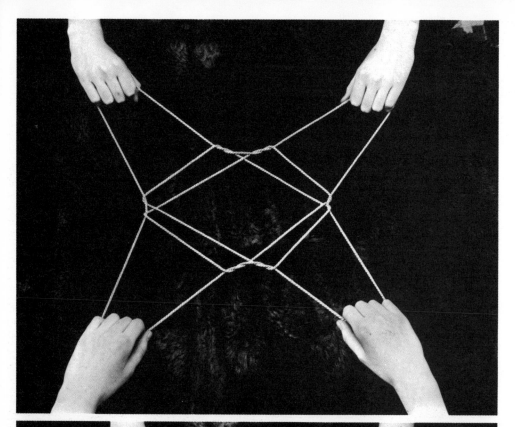

For two people

A string figure from the Wardaman tribe in northern Australia. (Obviously the order of movements for **B** is reversed as **B** is standing opposite **A**.)

A does opening A.

B puts both hands behind the front line as far as the wrists, bends the little fingers between the front crossed lines from above and between the back crossed lines from below. Hold the two index finger lines between the little fingers and the ring fingers on both sides.

A frees the index fingers and little fingers and puts these four fingers between the thumb lines so that they become wrist lines. On both sides, **A** takes hold of the loops which come from behind **B**'s little finger and ring finger, with the thumb and index finger. Pull the front line towards you.

B takes hold of the lines between the little finger and ring finger with the thumb and index finger.

A and **B** do a Navaho leap with the wrist line over both hands. Pull the lines tight.

A and **B** from below, put the three free fingers and then the index fingers of both hands into the corner loops and take them on to the wrists.

A takes the upper line which runs perpendicular to his own outer wrist lines and gives it to **B**. **A** takes hold of the corresponding line which is perpendicular to **B**'s wrist lines with the thumbs and index fingers of both hands and pulls it under the others.

A and **B** pull the wrists out of their loops and pull the lines they are holding through them. The hawk is completed but it is possible to weave another string through (see page 119).

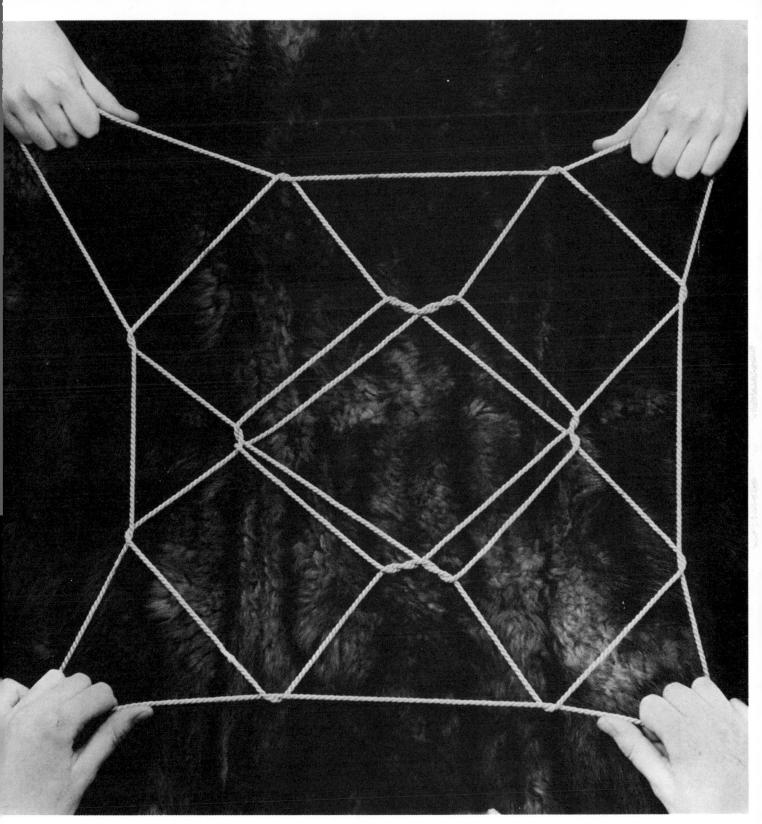

The Spider's Web

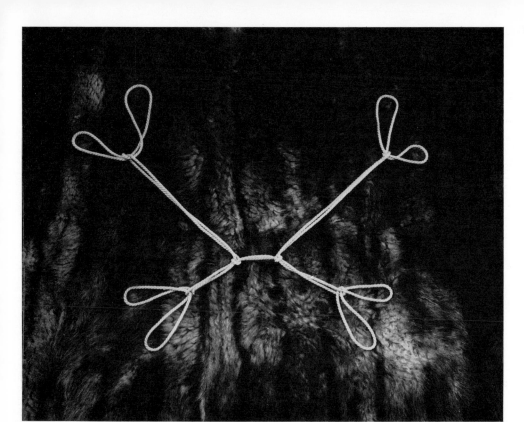

The Pepper Plant which is described at its last stage on page 195 (photograph 3) has been elaborated with a straight piece of string that is simply pulled through all the loops.

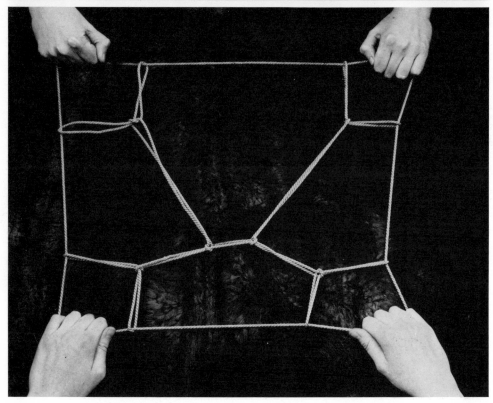

The Firmament

The Starry Sky (see pages 122–3) has been
extended with a second string circle, as in
the example of The Stickleback (see pages
114–16).

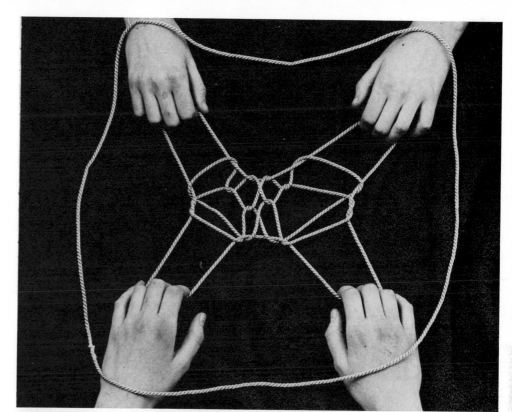

The Starry Sky

The Starry Sky often gave the Navaho Indians ideas for the names of their string figures; they lived in highland areas where clear night skies were common.

– Do opening A.
– Bend the thumbs over the front crossed lines, between the back crossed lines, under the front little finger lines, and pull these towards you. Pull the string tight.
– Bend the middle fingers over the index finger lines and from below put them behind the back thumb lines and pull them back.
– Free the thumbs.
– From above, put the thumbs into the index finger loops, under all the other lines and pull the back little finger line towards you on the thumbs.

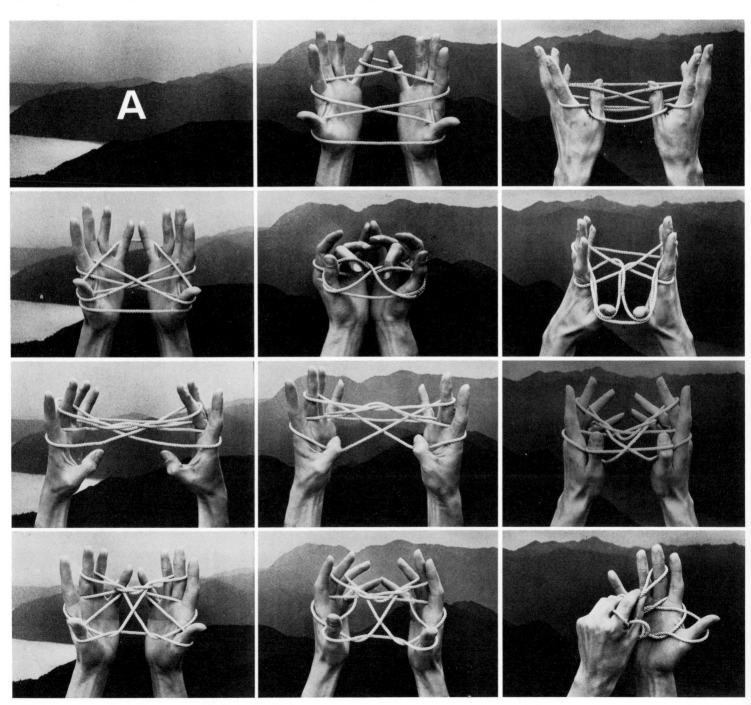

122

– Free the little fingers.
– With the right hand take the loop off the left middle finger, turn it half a turn in a clockwise direction and lay it round the left thumb and index finger. Do the same on the right hand, turning the loop half a turn in an anti-clockwise direction.

– Do a Navaho leap over both thumbs. Do a Navaho leap over both index fingers.
– Press the thumb loops (which you have just passed over) down with the thumbs, turn the thumbs towards you and stretch out the figure. If necessary, slide the loops on the index fingers up a little (see pages 124–5).

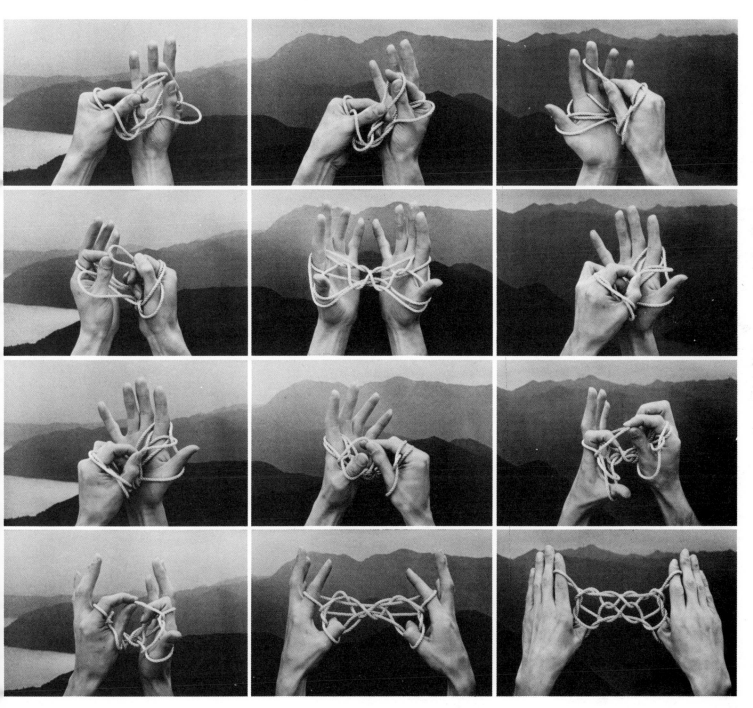

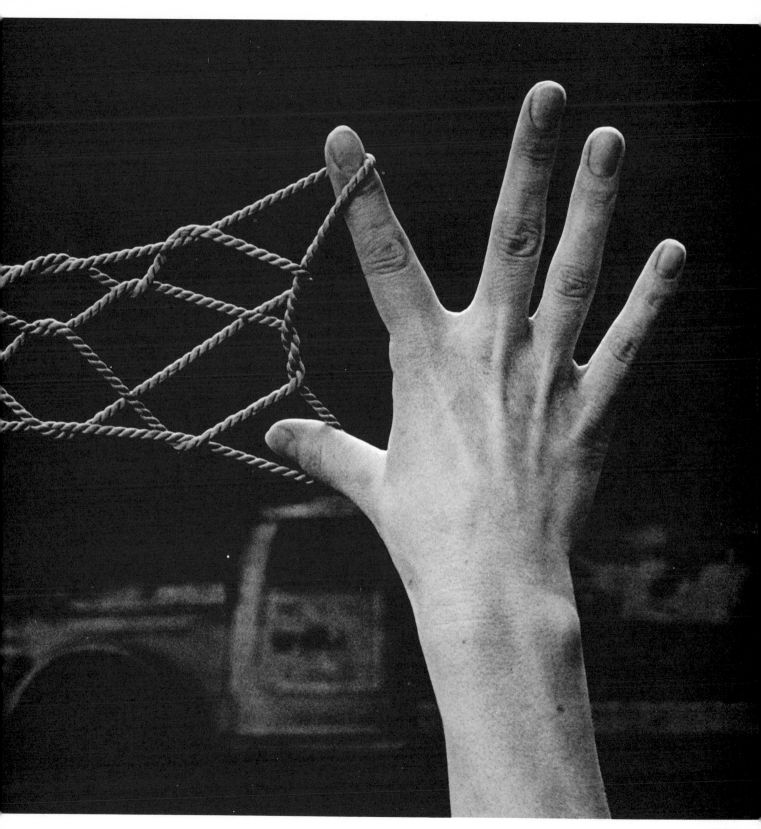

The Siberian Hut

Two men live in this little hut, which was originally an Eskimo figure. Suddenly a bear appears and the men run away in opposite directions.

– Do opening A.

– Hold all the crossed lines securely and throw the front line over both hands.

– Stretch the hands, put the thumbs between the front crossed lines and pull the bottom back line towards you on the thumbs.

– Do a Navaho leap over both hands. Spread the hands: this is a Siberian hut. The bear growls (you free the index fingers) and the men run away.

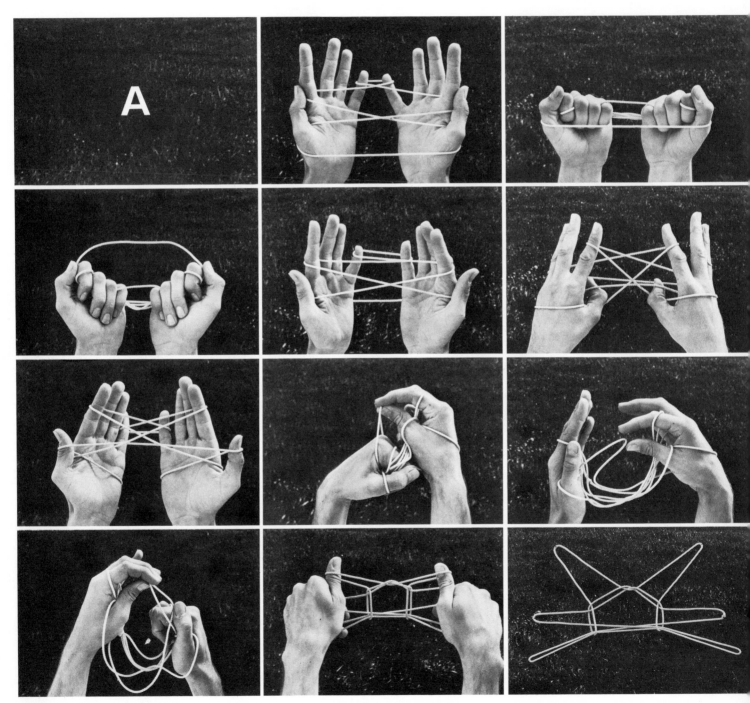

The Pole Star

Do opening A, keeping the lines tight. Bend the thumbs away from you over the back thumb lines, under the front ones and back up and towards you.

– Take the loop from the left little finger, give it a complete turn in an anti-clockwise direction and lay it back around the little finger. Do the same on the right, giving it a complete turn in a clockwise direction.
– Slide the index finger loops up, put the thumbs in the little finger loops from below

and pull the front little finger lines towards you.
– From above, put the little fingers through the index finger loops and from below into the thumb loops, pull the back thumb lines back through the index finger loops.
– Free the index fingers and spread the hands (see pages 128–9).

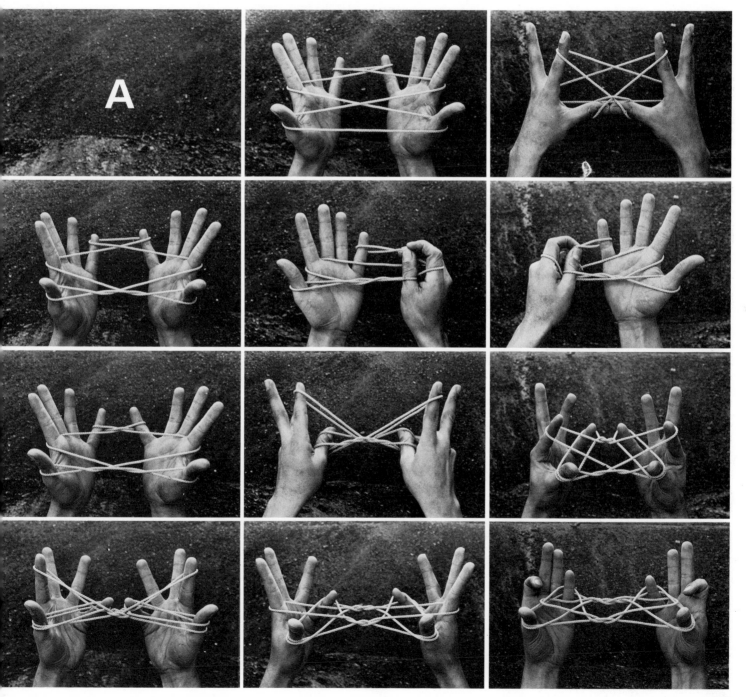

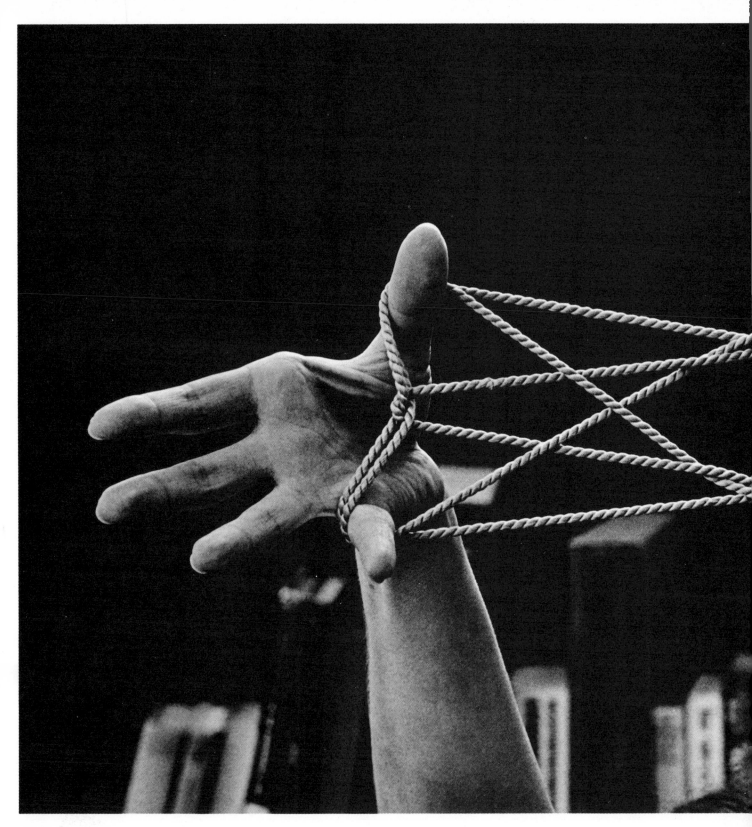

The Lotus Flower

This figure was discovered in 1923 in the New Hebrides in the Pacific. It is an interesting figure: a pyramid with a hexagonal base.

– Do opening A.
– Hold all the crossed lines securely and throw the front line back over both hands.
– Stretch the hands. From behind, put the thumbs between the front crossed lines, bend them towards you, then under all the lines. Then put them between the wrist and back

little finger line from behind and pull the latter towards you.
– Let the left thumb loop slide off, put the left thumb into the right thumb loop from below and pull the string tight.
– From below, put the little fingers in the index finger loops and free the index fingers.

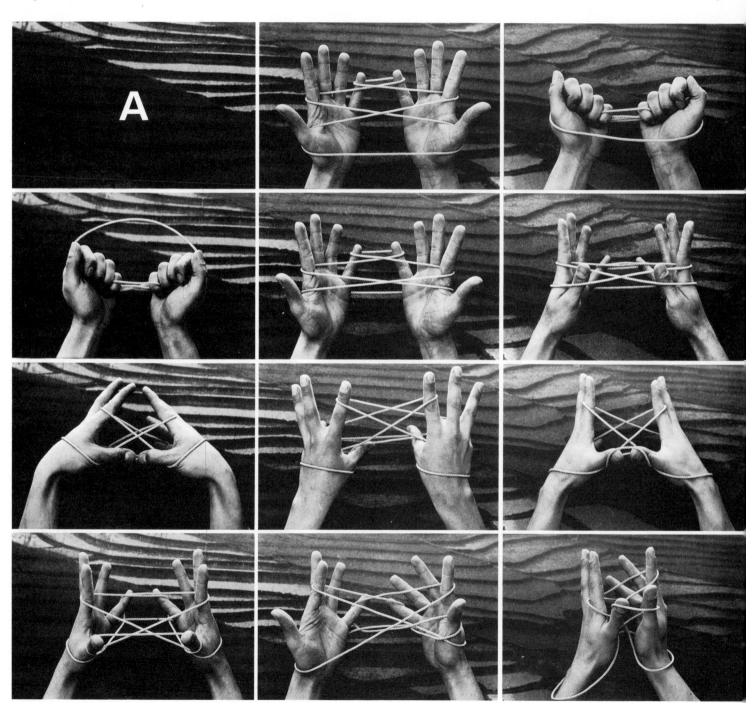

· From below, put the little fingers in the thumb loops and lay the back thumb lines under the two small little finger loops.
· Pass these small little finger loops on to the index fingers.
· Free the little fingers and thumbs and you will see the lotus flower blossom.

The Rabbit

This string figure originated amongst the Klamath Indians.
– Do opening A.
– Bend the index fingers and middle fingers of both hands towards you, over the index finger lines and the back thumb line and secure the front line between the two fingers

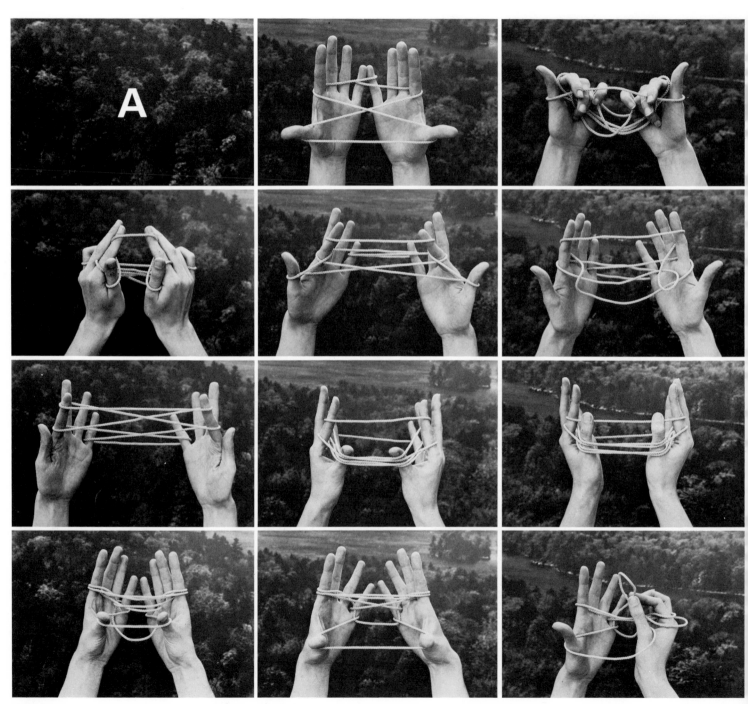

132

with the middle fingers at the bottom. Lift this line, give it half a turn and lay it around the index fingers.

– Free the thumbs.

– Bend the thumbs under the front line and the four crossed lines and pull these four lines under the straight index finger line towards you.

– Press the front, straight index finger line down with the thumbs below the back line and let the other four lines slide off the thumbs (keeping the lines taut). Pull the back line towards you on the thumbs.

– Lay the small index finger loops round the thumbs.

– Turn the thumbs inwards and down and do a Navaho leap over the thumbs.

– Free the little fingers.

– Put the four fingers into the thumb loops, lift the front thumb lines with the index fingers and you will see the rabbit.

133

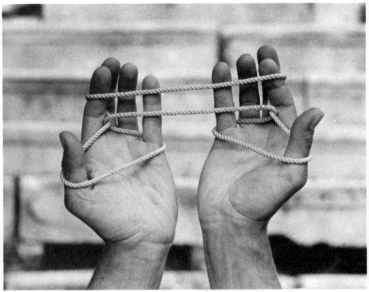

Would You Like a Sweet?

This amusing trick comes from northern Australia where it is known as Would You Like a Yam? (a sweet potato, the staple diet of the region).
– Do first position 1.
– Bend the index fingers down under the back line and towards you, lift it on to the fingertips.
– From below, put the thumbs behind the line between the top of the index finger and little finger, pull it towards you, under the front line.
– Bend the little fingers over the back index finger line, under the front long line and pull it back.
– Pull the front line towards you on the thumbs.
– With the right thumb and index finger take the loop off the left index finger and hold it between the left thumb and index finger.
– Ask an observer 'Would you like a sweet?' handing him the loop. As soon as he makes a grab for it, you pull on it with the right hand and the sweet disappears. (The left hand is completely free.) You can then do the same with the right hand.

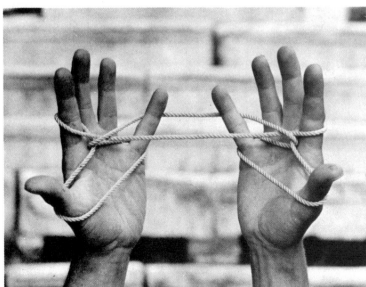

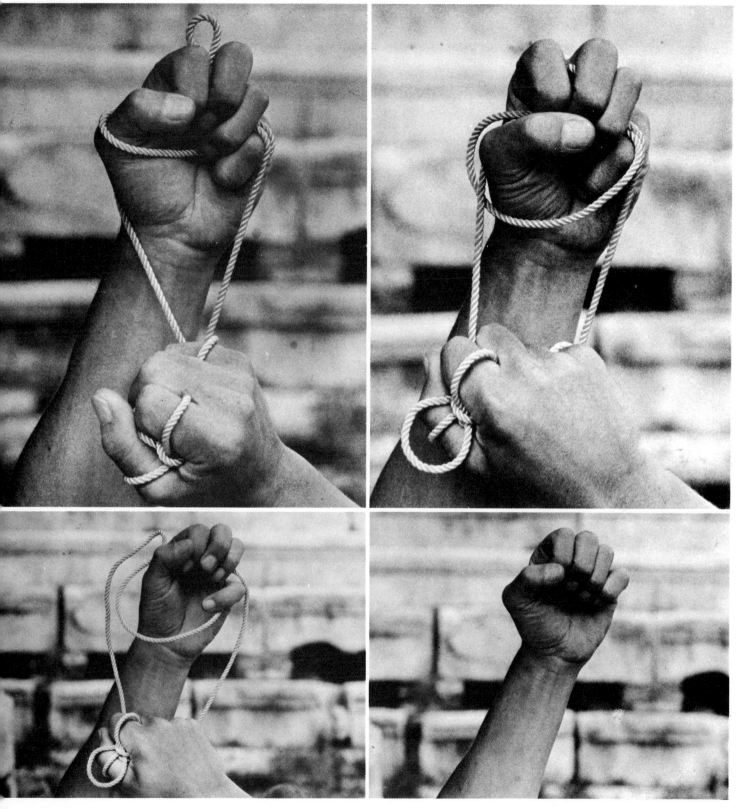

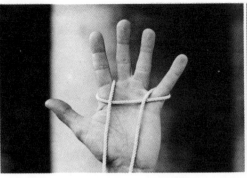  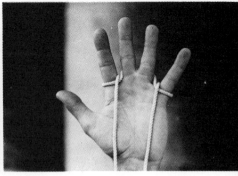

The Candle Thief

Sometimes string figures tell a story such as this folk tale which was known in many places in the last century, especially in England, Ireland and Germany. It dates from the time that wax candles were still made by hanging a bundle of cotton wicks in liquid wax. It is a sort of puppet show and

the story goes like this:
Once upon a time there was a man who had stolen a bundle of candles.

– Turn the left palm up and lay the string circle over the four fingers. Take hold of the two hanging lines with the right hand, and pass the front line up between the little

 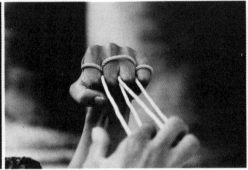 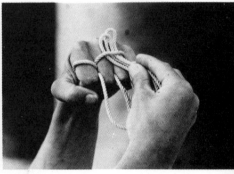

finger and the ring finger, and the back line up between the index finger and the middle finger. Raise the hand.

– Lay the line which runs across the hand between the hanging lines behind the middle finger and ring finger.

– With the right index finger and little finger

pull the loops of the left index finger and little finger towards you and hold them.

– From above, bend the ring finger into the little finger loop, bend the middle finger into the index finger loop so that the little finger is behind the back line and the index finger is in front of the front line.

– Clench the fist.

– From above, put the loops of the right hand through the loop at the back of the middle finger and ring finger, pull them tight.

– Lay the loop at the back of the ring finger and middle finger over both fingers on the

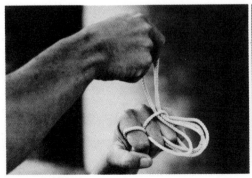  

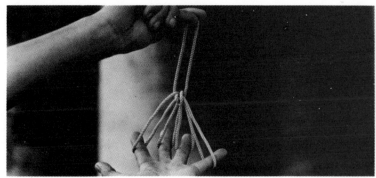

inside and pull the loop tight with the right index finger: this is the bundle of candles.
The thief took the bundle of candles home and hung them on a nail. (That is the index finger which you used to pull out the loop.)
He was absolutely exhausted after this theft.
– Lay the loop on the right index finger

round the left thumb. From below, take the loops at the back of the ring finger and middle finger of the left hand with the index finger and middle finger of the right hand.
He sat down in his easy chair . . .
– Pull the loops tight, hold them over the cupped palm; this is the chair.

. . . and fell asleep. When he woke up it was dark. So he went to fetch a pair of scissors to cut off a candle.
– Free the left thumb and make a scissor movement with the index finger and middle finger of the right hand: you will see the string scissors cutting.

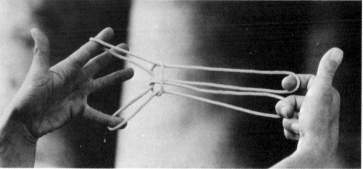

Just as he was doing this, a constable appeared – the thief was his only customer.
– Free the left index finger and pull: this is the constable's truncheon.
The constable politely knocked on the door with his truncheon and walked straight in. He didn't want to be too polite, after all. When he

saw the candles . . .
– Put the left hand in the left little finger loop as far as the wrist; free the right index finger, slide the knot to the middle and put the right hand in the right middle finger loop.
   . . . he immediately handcuffed the thief and

said, 'Come along with me. I'm on my own at the station . . .'

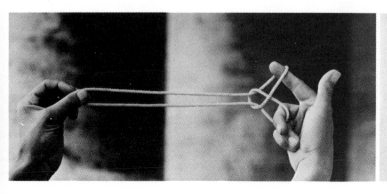

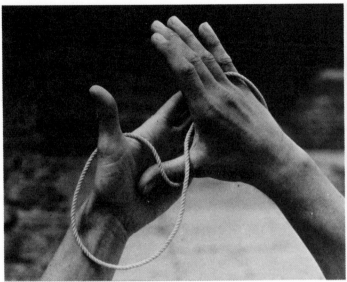 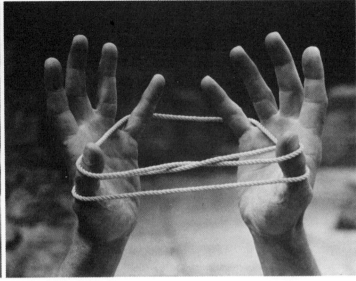

The Tinder-box

This string figure comes from the Caroline Islands in Polynesia, and is made with a short (or doubled) string circle.
- Do first position 1.
- From above, put the right thumb behind the line on the left palm and pull (the back is visible).
- Put the left thumb under the diagonal line between the left little finger and right thumb and pull the string taut.
- Take the back thumb lines on to the index fingers.
- Do a Navaho leap over both thumbs.
- Free the little fingers.
- Turn the palms away from you, bend the left hand forwards and down, and up again in front of the right hand. Move the right hand to the left and turn both palms towards you.

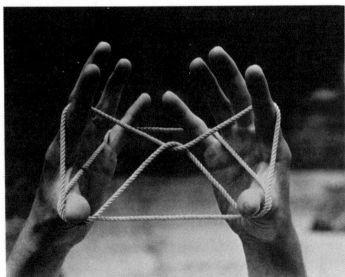 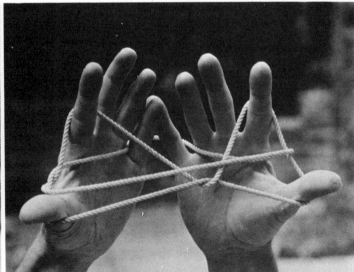

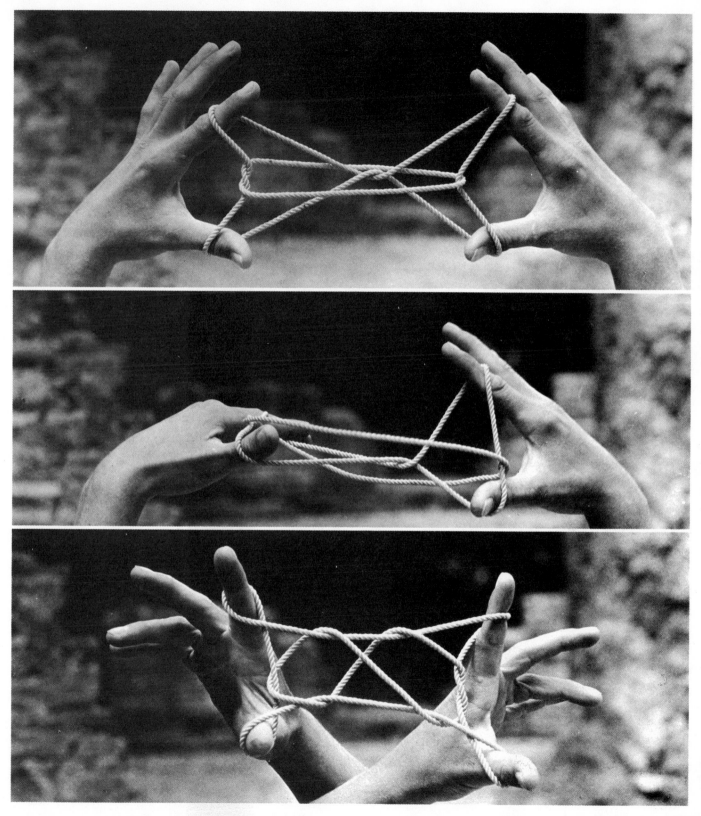

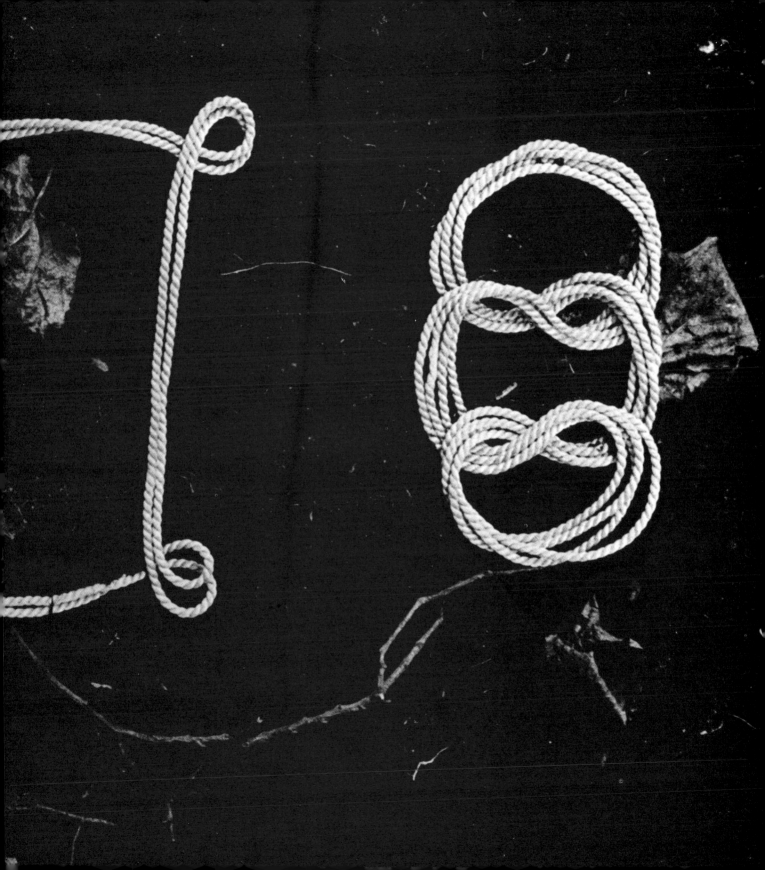

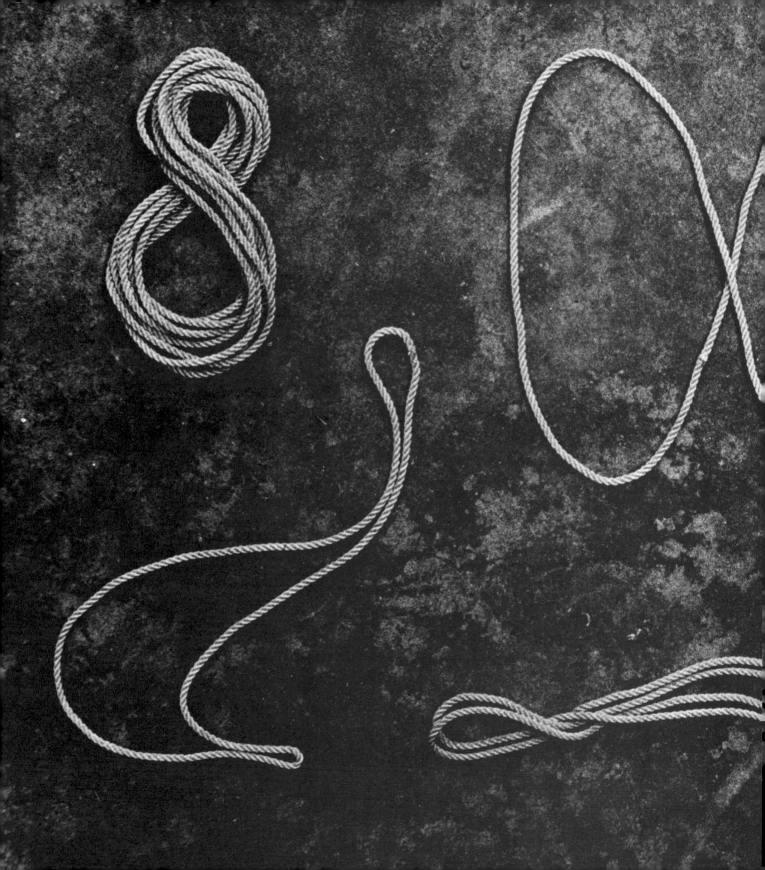

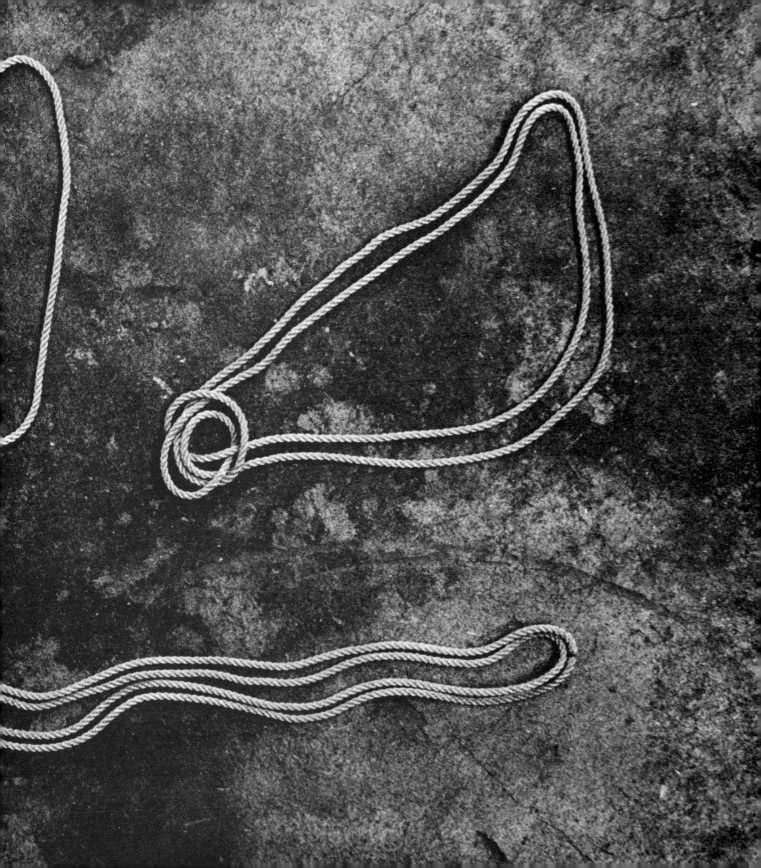

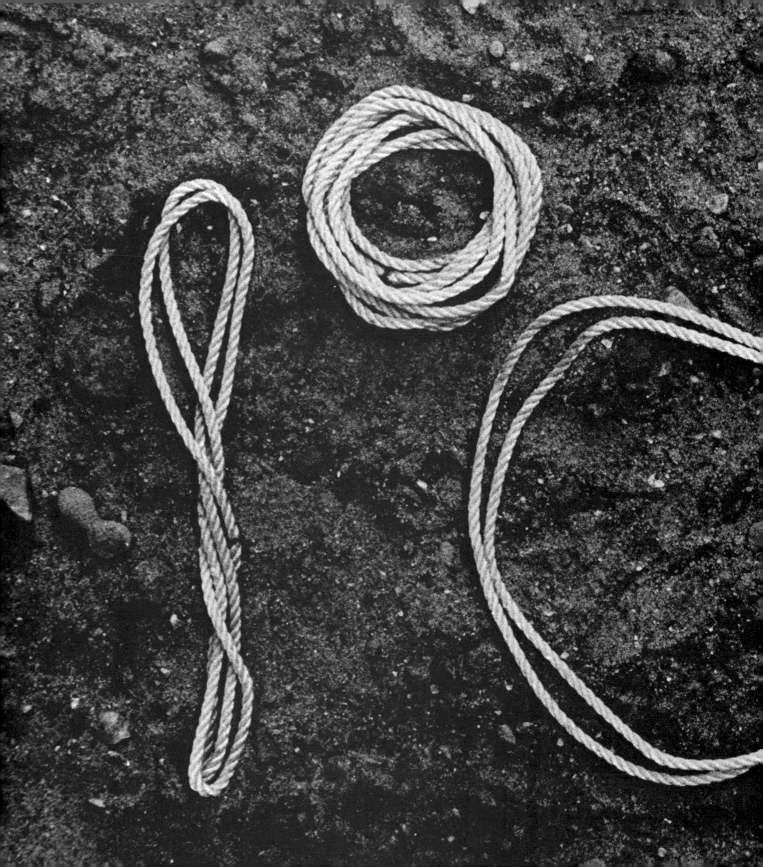

Look, a piece of string on the ground

String and the Woman

Even though you may not pick up a piece of string in the Yirrkalla region, you may certainly look at it. McCarthy describes other things apart from making string figures on the fingers or using string to do tricks; the people also lay out extremely expressive figures on the ground. Twelve of these figures are shown on the preceding pages. Some of them are obviously a very personal expression, but most of them are universal.

Pages 140 and 141 from left to right: Dabbling Ducks, The Octopus's Cave in the Rocks and Three Vulvas.
Pages 142 and 143 from left to right (top): A Bee, Two Bananas, Cockerel Scratching in the Dust, (below) Runaway Dog and The Snail.
Pages 144 and 145 from left to right: Point of a Spear, Anus, A Goose and The Coconut Palm.
  It might be a good idea to let your imagination work on these, just as the people from Yirrkalla did, expressing what they saw around them.
Page 147: Wasps' Nest, a string figure that is not made on the fingers or the ground, but is twisted around the ear, from northern Queensland.

Our 'civilization' has stamped out and repressed the indigenous culture of those people we think of as 'primitive'. The strength of these cultures is shown by the fact that even today string games continue to be played; they have a social and often a magical significance we can barely hope to comprehend. Very understandably the string circle repeatedly turns out to be a symbol for the female sex.

In about 1948 Frederick McCarthy investigated string figures and their significance in northern Australia. He described a number of 'laws' in regard to string that the inhabitants of the Yirkalla have to comply with:

'... If a boy or a young unmarried man passes a village and picks up a piece of string that has been lost or thrown away by a woman, he may be punished for it by her husband. The man has every right to suspect him of having a sexual relationship with his wife. Only the men of the woman's immediate family may touch her string.

If a man drops a piece of string and a woman picks it up it means that she has a relationship with the owner of the string.

If a woman gives her string to a man it means that she wants to sleep with him. If her husband finds out he has the right to punish her.

If a woman accepts a piece of string from a man and hides it in her shoulder-bag it means that she feels attracted to him and would not be unwilling to meet him in the forest. If her husband sees the string and finds out who the owner is he will challenge him to a duel with spears and has the right to kill him.

If a man steals some string from a woman he can be sure her husband will seek revenge, for the latter may assume that the man secretly loves his wife or wishes to enchant her.'

So if you go to Australia, it's obviously not a good idea to lose your own string and probably advisable to keep your hands off other people's.

1. Two Bananas	7. Dabbling Ducks
2. A Scratching Cockerel	8. Coconut Palm
3. A Bee	9. The Snail
4. Anus	10. Runaway Dog
5. Point of a Spear	11. The Octopus's C
6. Three Vulvas	12. A Goose

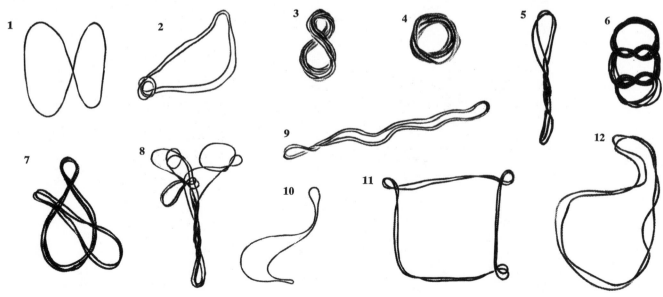

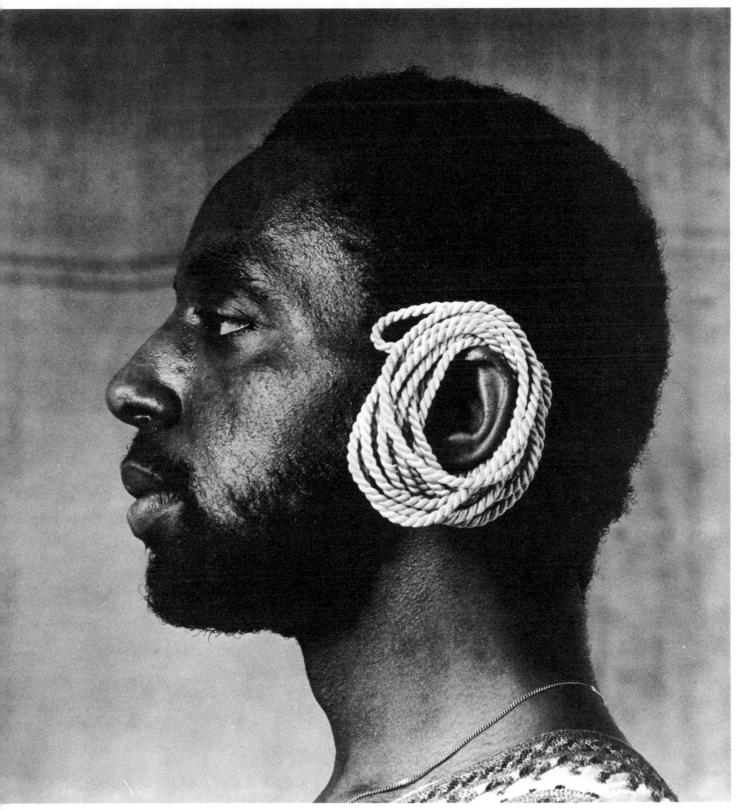

The Diadem

This string figure is very common and is known under many different names: Jacob's Ladder, The Gate, Four Eyes, The Hair-net, Four Diamonds or Osage Diamonds.
– Do opening A.
– Free the thumbs.
– Bend the thumbs under all the lines and pull the back line towards you on the thumbs.
– Bend the thumbs over the front index finger line, put them between the crossed lines from below and pull the back index finger line towards you.
– Free the little fingers.

148

Bend the little fingers over the index finger line and put them into the thumb loops from below and pull the back thumb lines back on the little fingers.

– Free the thumbs.

– Bend the thumbs over the index finger loops, put them into the little finger loops from below and pull the front little finger lines towards you.

– From below, put the thumbs into the index finger loops next to the index fingers and pull the string taut.

– Do a Navaho leap over both thumbs.

– From above, put the index fingers into the triangles next to the thumbs and bend the hands inwards. (The little fingers are automatically freed.) Turn the palms away from you and spread the diadem out on the thumbs and index fingers (see page 150).

Girl with The Diadem.

Sunset

This figure is well-known in the island of Murray, where it is known as *Lem Baraigida* ('sunset').

It requires a string circle about 3 metres long.

– Do opening A.
– Bend the little fingers over the crossed lines, under the front thumb line and pull this back.
– Free the thumbs.
– Bend the thumbs under the four crossed lines and pull the front little finger lines towards you.
– Free the little fingers.

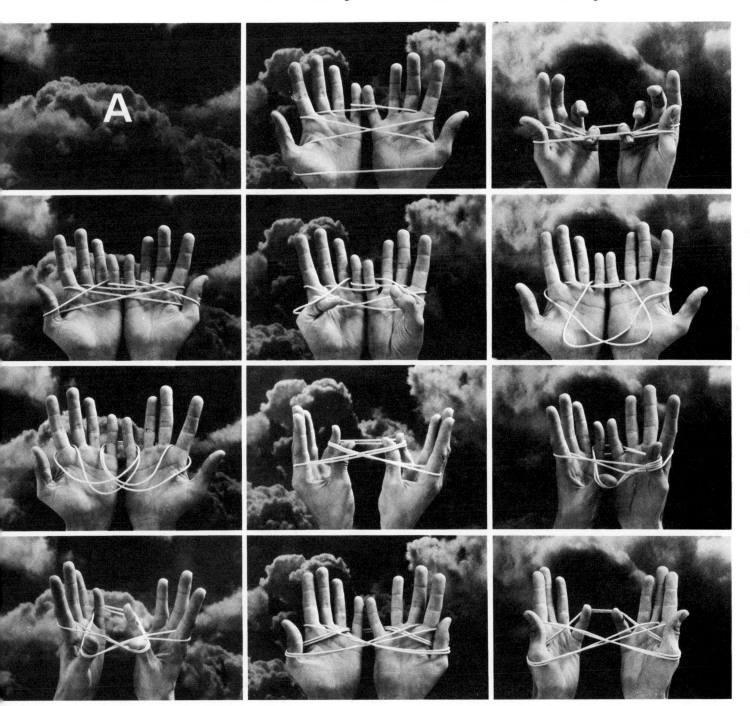

– Bend the little fingers over the index finger loops and from below put them into the double thumb loops. Pull the back thumb line back.

– Pass the right index finger loop on to the left index finger and pass the original left index finger loop over the other one and lay

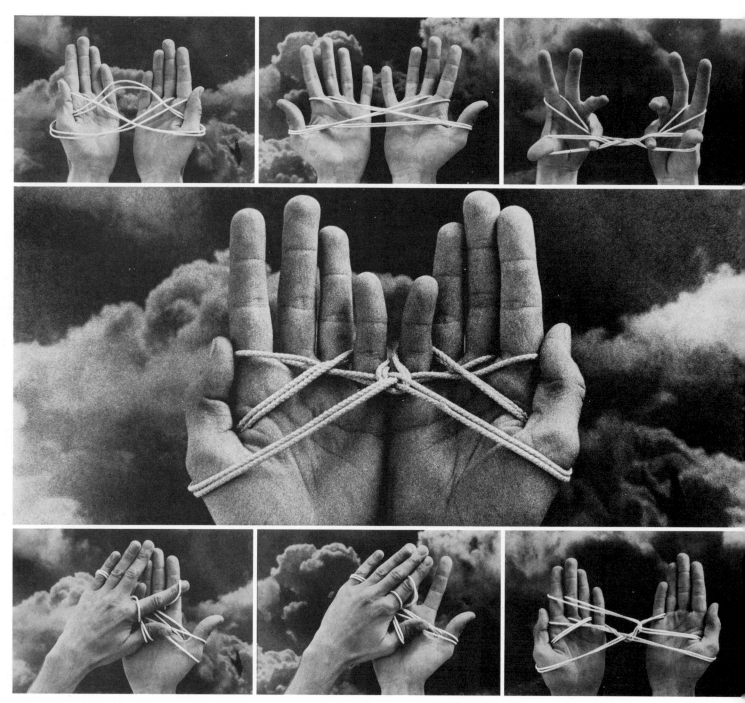

it around the right index finger.
– From above, put the middle fingers in the index finger loops and put them into the double thumb loops from below. Pull the thumb loops completely through the index finger loops.
– Free the thumbs.

– Free the index fingers.
– From below, put the thumbs into the double middle finger loops and pass these loops over on to the thumbs.
– There are now four diagonals across the middle of the figure; slide them apart and you will see a small triangle with the point

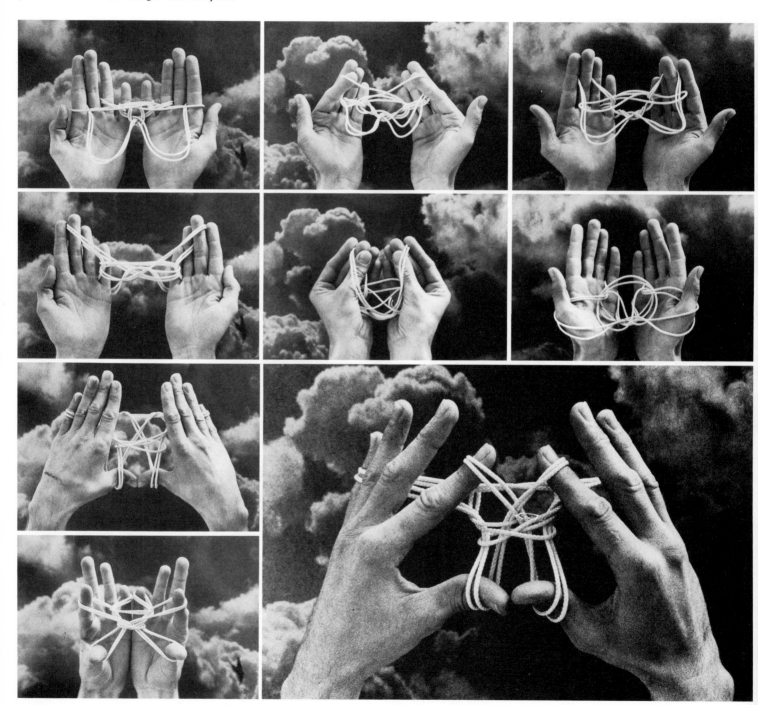

towards you. Put the index fingers into the 'eyes' next to this triangle and then put them into it from below and pull the side lines of the triangle over the index fingers.
– From above, put the middle fingers through the index finger loops and from below, through the thumb loops and pull these entirely through the index finger loops.
– Free the thumbs.
– Free the index fingers.
– Divide the loops on both hands over four fingers and you can see the rays of the setting sun.

Headhunters

This string figure describes the legendary struggle between the inhabitants of the island of Murray and the inhabitants of the neighbouring island of Daoear. The heads of the conquered tribe were taken to Murray as trophies, and this is where the string figure originates.

– Do opening A.
– Bend the little fingers over all the crossed lines, put them under the front thumb line and take the thumb loops on to the little fingers.
– Bend the thumbs under the index finger loops, put them into the little finger loops

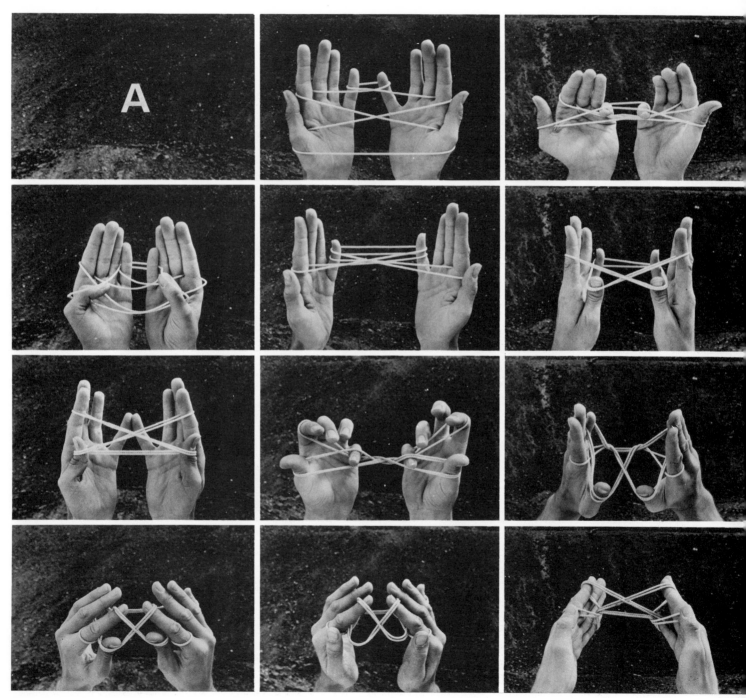

d pass the double little finger loops to the
umbs.
Bend the little fingers over the index finger
ops, put them into the thumb loops from
low and pull the back double thumb lines
ck.
Bend the fingertips together and from

below, put the index fingers into the enclosed
triangle in the middle of the figure. Pull the
side lines of the triangle over the index
fingers.
– Free the thumbs.
– Do a Navaho leap over both index fingers.
– Bend the index fingers down, towards you

and up again.* Repeat this a few times so
that the index finger loops stand up.
– Free the index fingers and put the other
fingers in the little finger loops. The
headhunters are now ready for the fray.
– Gradually pull the hands apart and you will
see the fighters attack. One will lose his head.

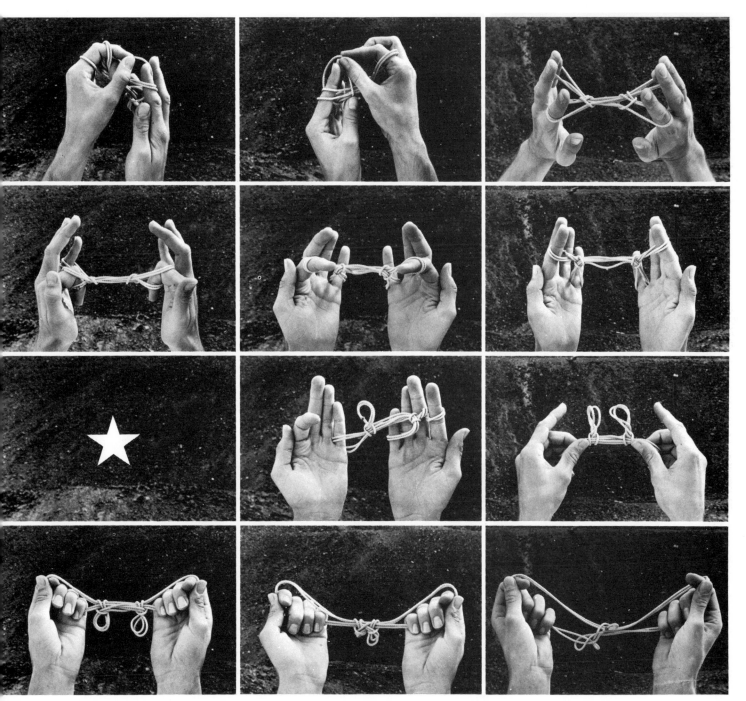

157

The game of small changes

All the examples of string figures shown in this book were thought up a long time ago by people all over the world: Eskimos, Indians or Maoris. Fingers have good memories, so after a little practice, you will know a whole series of figures and tricks by heart and will be able to amaze your friends with them.

However, this is only the beginning.

Many figures in this book have been passed on from father to son, and from mother to daughter since time immemorial.

There is no way of being sure that the figures thought up by distant ancestors are exactly the same as the ones we do now. For once you've mastered the technique of these string games and your fingers have learned to do what you are thinking, it really becomes fun. You start discovering possibilities and new variations for yourself, which is what has been happening for generations. Sometimes these variations have been passed on, as in the riddle game Tunah, Tunah which appears in a few pages. A little

later the 'new' variation has become part of the tradition. But usually the secret remains yours. It is worth a try. The following pages show what a big difference a small change can make in The Apache Door or The Diadem. Hein Broos, who has collected many other string figures from all over the world, gives many examples of how a completely different figure can be made with just one or two changes.

Tangarot

This series of string figures comes from the Eskimos in the north-east part of Siberia, near the Bering Straits: the Tangarot. Jenness described them in his travel diary of an expedition to the Tanga district and Alaska.

- Do the ribcage opening.
- Secure all the lines except for the front ones and throw the front line back over the hands.
- Put the thumbs in front of the index fingers on either side of the crossover, take them under all the other lines and pull the wrist line towards you.
- Do a Navaho leap over four fingers of both hands with the lines running across the back of the hand (photograph 1).
- This is the house where the Tangarot people live; when the house collapses (by pulling the index fingers (photograph 2) and then the middle fingers (photograph 3) out of their loops), the people run out (pull the ring fingers out of their loops and pull) (photograph 4).

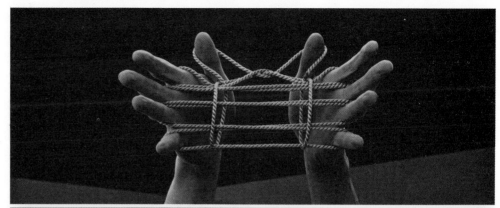

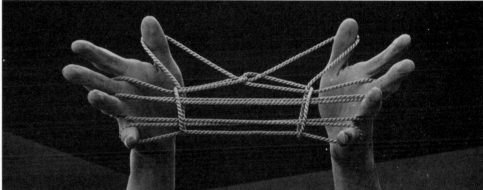

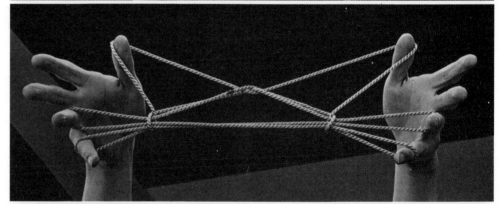

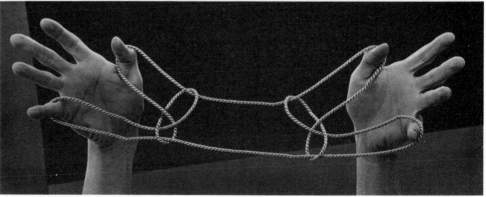

Sardines

A continuous figure from the South Sea Islands.

– Do a Navaho opening and turn the palms upwards.

– From above, put the little fingers into the index finger loops and pull the front index finger line back.

– Free the index fingers.

– From below, put the thumbs behind the front little finger line and pull it towards you.

– Do a Pindiki stroke with the back thumb line. This is The Calm Sea at Low Tide (photograph 1).

– Free the thumbs, turn the palms of the hands away; the fingers should be pointing upwards.

– Bend the thumbs behind all the lines and put them between the index finger lines. Pull the back index finger line under all the lines towards you. Stretch the hands.

– Free the index fingers.

– Put the thumbs in the little finger loops and pull the front little finger lines towards you.

– Do a Pindiki stroke with the back thumb line.

– These are The Two Sardines (photograph 2).

Sardines tend to multiply very quickly.

– Turn the palms of the hands away and repeat the movements from The Calm Sea as often as you can. Every time there will be two new sardines.

It is also possible to catch sardines.

– Pull the index fingers back and turn the whole figure round: take the two front thumb lines from the left thumb between the teeth and free the left hand. From above, put the left thumb and little finger into the loops of the corresponding fingers on the right hand and pass them on.

– Take the mouth loops on the right side between the finger and thumb of the left hand, let go of the mouth loops, turn the left hand straight and put the right thumb and little finger into the loops from the front.

– Repeat the movements from The Calm Sea.

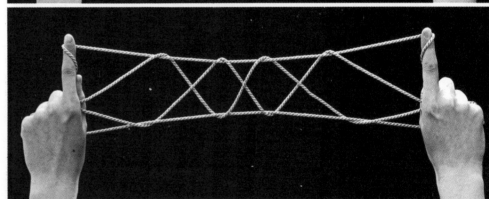

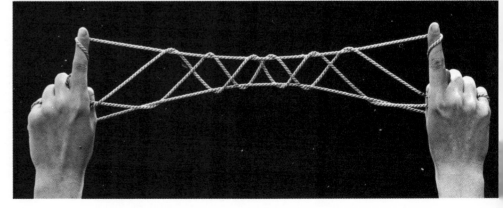

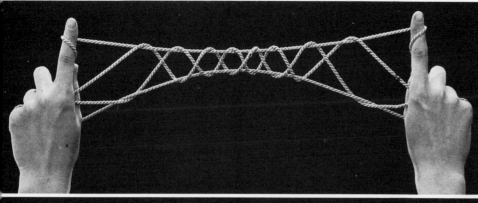

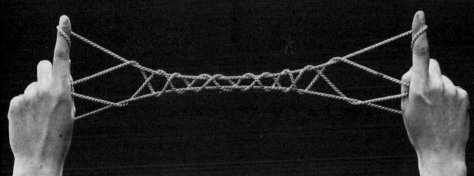

The Diadem

(See the photographs on pages 162–3.)

Photograph 1

1 Do opening A.
2 Free the thumbs.
3 Bend the thumbs under all the lines and pull the back little finger line towards you.
4 Bend the thumbs over the front index finger line and from below put them between the crossed lines, pull the back index finger line towards you.
5 Free the little fingers.
6 Bend the little fingers over the index finger line and put them under the back thumb line and pull it back.
7 Free the thumbs.
8 Bend the thumbs over the index finger loops, under the front little finger lines and pull them towards you.
9 From below, put the thumbs into the small index finger loops next to the index fingers and pull the string taut.
10 Do a Navaho leap over both thumbs.
11 From above, put the index fingers into the loop which has just been passed over, over the line above it, and do the turning stroke. Free the little fingers and stretch out the diadem.

First Variation (Photograph 2)
– Carry out movements 1–8.
– With the thumb and index finger of the right hand take hold of the loop on the left index finger behind the diagonal and turn it once round in an anti-clockwise direction. Lay the loop back around the index finger.
– Do the same on the left turning it round in a clockwise direction.
– Carry out movements 9–11.

Second Variation (Photograph 3)
– Carry out movements 1 and 2.
– Bend the thumbs under the front line, put them between the crossed lines from above, under the front little finger lines and pull them towards you.
– Bend the thumbs over the index finger loops, under the back line and pull it towards you.

– Do a Navaho leap over the thumbs.
– Carry out movements 9–11.

Third Variation (Photograph 4)
– Carry out movements 1 and 2.
– Bend the thumbs under the front line and the crossed lines, under the front little finger lines and pull them towards you.
– From above, put the thumbs into the index finger loops and pull the back index finger lines towards you.
– Do a Navaho leap over both thumbs.
– Bend the thumbs over the double line, under the back line and pull it towards you.
– Do a Navaho leap over both thumbs.
– Carry out movements 9–11.

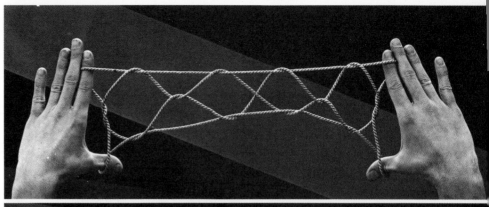

Fourth Variation (Photograph 5)
– Carry out movements 1 and 2.
– Bend the thumbs under the index finger loops and pull the back index finger line towards you.
– Bend the thumbs over the index finger line, put them under the front little finger lines and pull these lines towards you.
– Do a Navaho leap over both thumbs.
– Carry out movements 9–11.

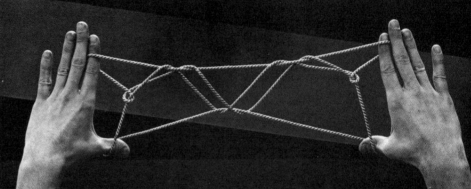

Fifth Variation (Photograph 6)
– Carry out movements 1 and 2.
– Bend the thumbs under the index finger lines and the front little finger line and pull this last line towards you.
– Bend the thumbs over the index finger lines and put them under the back line and pull it towards you.
– Do a Navaho leap over both thumbs.
– Take hold of the loop on the left index finger behind the diagonal with the thumb and index finger of the right hand and give it a complete turn in a clockwise direction; lay the loop back around the index finger.
– Do the same on the right hand, turning it around in an anti-clockwise direction.
– Carry out movements 9–11.

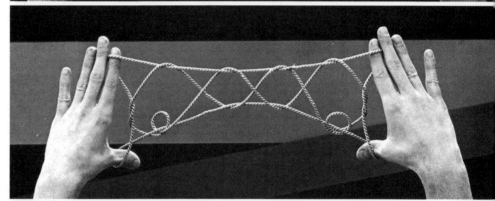

Sixth Variation (Photograph 7)
– Carry out movements 1 and 2.
– Bend the thumbs under the front line, put them between the crossed lines from above and pull the front little finger lines towards you.
– Bend the thumbs over the front index finger line, under the back index finger line and pull it towards you.
– Do a Navaho leap over the thumbs.
– Bend the thumbs over the double line,

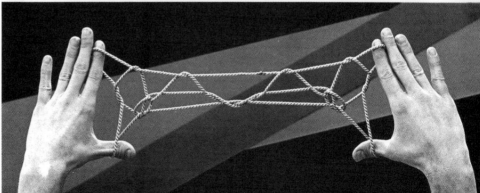

...der the back line and pull it towards you.
Do a Navaho leap over the thumbs.
Carry out movements 9–11.

...venth Variation (Photograph 8)
Carry out movements 1 and 2.
Bend the thumbs under the front line and
...e crossed lines and pull the front little
...nger lines towards you.
Bend the thumbs over the front index
...nger line, under the back index finger line,
...nder the back line and pull this towards
...ou.
Do a Navaho leap over both thumbs.
Carry out movements 9–11.

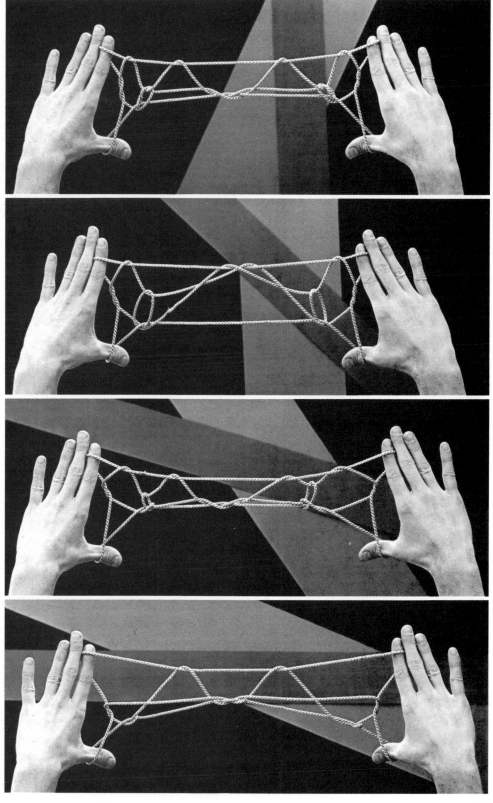

163

Tunah, Tunah

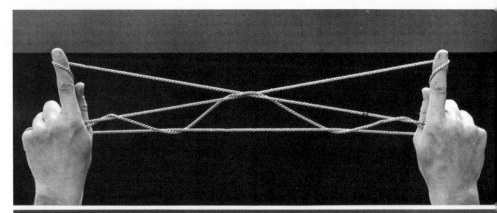

Photograph 1

A riddle game from the Gilbert Islands. (Repeated movements are indicated by letters.)

– Do a Navaho opening, turn the palms of the hands inwards.

– From below, put the little fingers between the index finger lines, over the front index finger lines down and under the back thumb lines: pull these back.

– Free the thumbs.

– From below, put the thumbs into the little finger loops, pull the front little finger lines down below the index finger loops and pull the front index finger line towards you. (D)

– Free the index fingers. (W)

– Do a Pindiki stroke with the back thumb line.

A song accompanies this movement:

'*Tunah, tunah, townah, townah,*
Ba akea kain waia,
Ba ti Na Oebwebwe – ao – aa – ee,
Ba ti Na Oemake – ao – aa – ee
Ba ti Kabane bai – ao – aa – ee.'

(Tunah, tunah, townah, townah, There is no one in the canoe except Ubwebwe, Umake or Kabane bai.) The observers guess which of these three local gods is represented by the string figure that is made.

Photograph 2

– Take the thumbs off the index fingers so that there are index finger loops and take the thumb away from underneath. (L)

– From above, put the thumbs into the index finger loops and pass these on to the thumbs. Do a Pindiki stroke. *Tunah, tunah . . .*

– Do L. From below, bend the thumbs behind the back index finger line and pull it under the front index finger lines. (T) Do W and a Pindiki stroke.

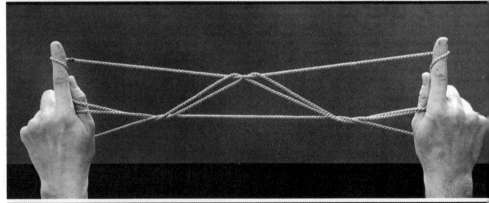

Photograph 3

– Do L, T, W and a Pindiki stroke consecutively – *Tunah, tunah . . .*

– Do L. Bend the thumbs into the index finger loops from above and pass these on to the thumbs. (O) Do a Pindiki stroke.

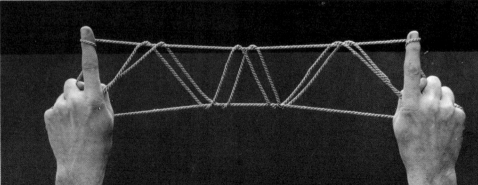

– Free the thumbs.
– Do O. From below, put the thumbs into the little finger loops and pull the front little finger lines towards you. Do a Pindiki stroke.

tunah, tunah …

– Do W. Take the lines between the thumbs and little fingers off the thumbs.
– From above, pass the thumb loops on to the index fingers. Do D, W and a Pindiki stroke.

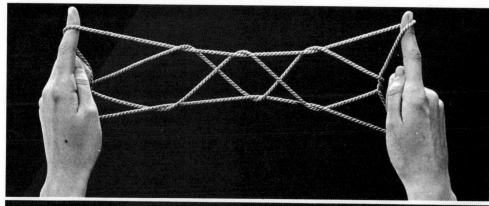

The Sunfish

– Do first position 1 on the right hand.
– From above, put the left index finger (with the back against the palm of the hand) behind the line running across the palm of the hand, pull the loop out and drop it.
– In the same way put the left index finger behind the line on the palm of the hand and pull it through the long loop.
– Do first position 1 on the left hand.
– Once more put the left index finger behind the line on the right palm in the same way, and then make half a turn towards you and so. Pull the lines tight.
– From above, put the right index finger in the right thumb loop, pull the back thumb line back to above the little finger loop, hook the right index finger from above into this loop, and turn the finger towards you and back up.
– Stretch the lines on the tops of the index fingers. Hook the base line of the triangle by the right index finger down with the little finger and let the little finger line slide off. With the left little finger hook down the back index finger line from above and let the little finger line slide off.
– Free the thumbs, stretch out the figure (photograph 1). Let an observer put his hand into an opening of this figure of The Sunfish (this is what the Papuans sometimes did with suspects) and pull the whole figure to one side: if the hand is freed, he is innocent.
– With the hands in the same position press

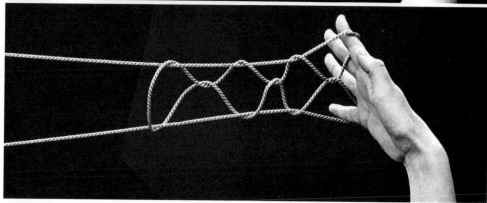

the base line of the triangles by the index fingers down with the thumbs below the diagonal lines underneath, hook them on to the back of the thumbs from below, stretch the little fingers and pass the line which was pressed down on to the back of the little fingers.
– Free the index fingers and spread the thumbs and little fingers (photograph 2).
– Put up the fingers and hook the index fingers behind the line which is at right angles to the thumb lines, pull it to the palm of the hand past the back thumb line and

take this on to the back of the index fingers.
– Free the thumbs.
– Put the thumbs behind the front index finger lines and pass the whole loop on to the thumbs.
– Put the index fingers between the two lines running from the palm of the hand to the middle, hook the front lines to the hand over the back thumb lines and pull these up on the back of the index fingers.
– Free the thumbs, spread the index fingers and little fingers, and carefully pull the lines taut: you will see a sea-cow swimming away.

The Apache Door

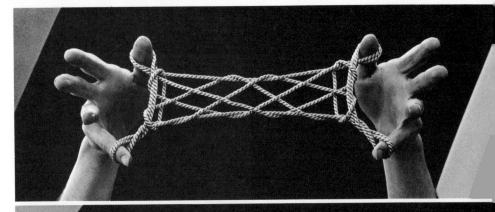

Photograph 1

1 Do first position 1.

2 Put the whole right hand under the line running across the left palm. Pull the string tight and do the same on the right with the left hand.

3 From below, put the thumbs into the little finger loops and pull the front little finger lines towards you.

4 From below, put the little fingers into the thumb loops and pull the back thumb lines back.

5 Slide the lines round the right thumb up, bend the right hand to the front, take the right thumb under all the lines and raise the thumb and hand up again. Take hold of the two loops on the thumb with the thumb and index finger of the left hand, take the thumb back and put it back into the loops, over all the lines. Do the same on the left.

6 Do a Navaho leap over the whole hands with the two wrist lines.

7 Pull the figure tight.

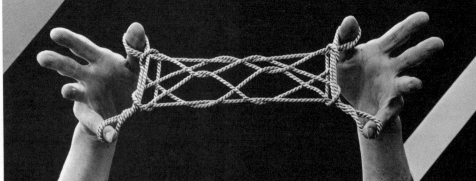

First Variation (Photograph 2)

– Do first position 1.

– From above, put the right hand under the line running across the left palm (with the palms facing inwards). Pull the string tight and do the same on the right.

– Carry out movements 3–7.

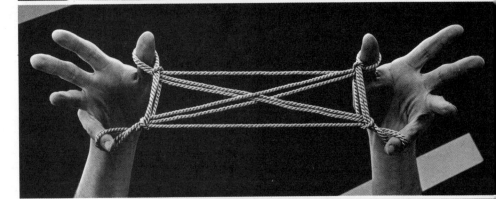

Second Variation (Photograph 3)

– Do first position 1.

– From above, put the right hand under the line running across the palm of the hand with the back of the hand against the palm of the left hand and turn the right hand back in an anti-clockwise direction. Do the same on the right, turning the hand in a clockwise direction.

– Carry out movements 3–7.

Third Variation (Photograph 4)

– Carry out movements 1 and 2.

– Turn the thumbs back under their own loops; first away from you and down, then up towards you.

Turn the little fingers under their own
ops; first towards you and down, then
way from you and up.
Carry out movements 3–7.

ourth Variation (Photograph 5)
Do first position 1.
From above, put the right hand under the
e running across the left palm, with the
ck of the hand against the left palm, and
rn the right hand back in a clockwise

direction. Do the same on the right, now
turn it back in an anti-clockwise direction.
– Turn the thumbs and little fingers under
their own loops (see third variation).
– Carry out movements 3–7.

Fifth Variation (Photograph 6)
– Do first position 1.
– From above, put the right index finger
behind the line on the left palm and turn it
back in a clockwise direction.

– Put the left index finger under the
crossover of the index finger lines and
behind the line across the right palm from
above, pull it out and turn the index finger
back in an anti-clockwise direction.
– Take the loop off the right index finger
and put it around the whole hand. Do the
same on the left.
– Turn the thumbs and little fingers under
their own loops (see third variation).
– Carry out movements 3–7.

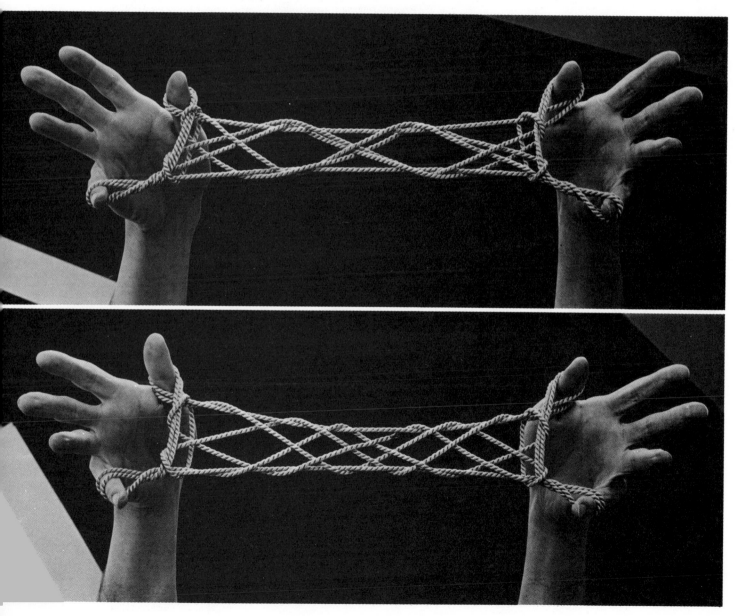

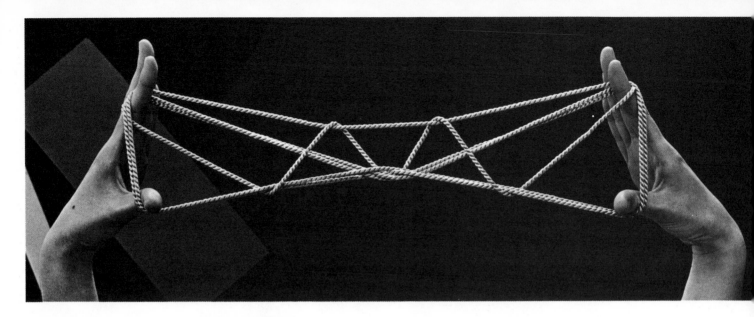

The Rock of Waondeli

The mysterious rock

When anthropologists are searching for string figures they sometimes come up against problems. In some cases an experienced string 'expert' is not particularly keen to perform a certain complicated string figure in painfully slow motion if he usually does it in a matter of seconds. It would be extremely boring for him. It would be like asking a famous concert pianist to play a piece note by note when he would usually play it really quickly. He would probably refuse. On the other hand there might be quite another reason for the string player's reluctance. The English anthropologist, Compton, found this on the island of Lifu in the Pacific. One of the inhabitants taught him a string figure but refused to give it a name. He would only say that it represented a 'mountain', but there are no mountains in Lifu. Compton was insistent and finally the man revealed the secret to this uninitiated anthropologist: it was the Rock of Waondeli, a coral reef with protruding peaks which lies in the sea in front of Lifu and where – the big secret – the evil spirit

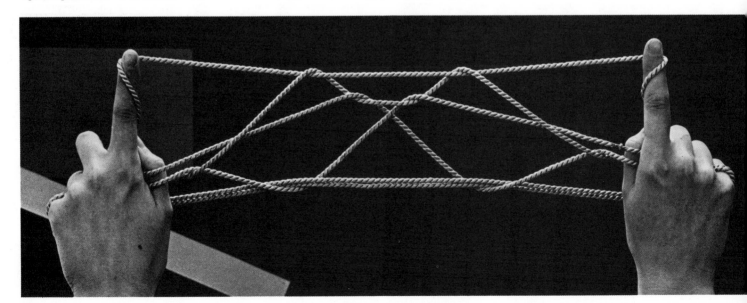

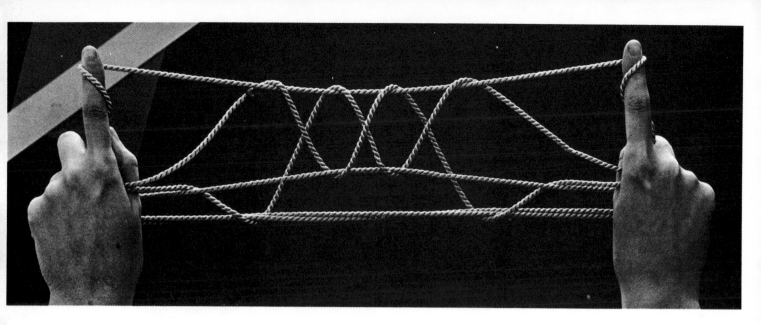

Waondeli lives.
– Do opening A.
– Bend the index fingers away from you over the back line, move them down under the little finger and index finger lines towards you and back up again, behind the back thumb lines.
– Bend the index fingers towards you, over the back thumb lines, down, away from you and back up.
– Free the thumbs.

– From above, put the index fingers behind the front little finger lines, move them down, towards you and back up.
– Put the thumbs behind the double line in front of the index fingers and pull them towards you.
– Free the little fingers (photograph 1).
– From below, bend the little fingers in front of the double diagonal line from behind the index fingers and pull them back.
– Free the index fingers.

– From behind, bend the index fingers under the back thumb line and do a Pindiki stroke (photograph 2).
– Free the index fingers, turn the palms towards you and do a Pindiki stroke with the back thumb line (photograph 3).
– Free the index fingers, bend the thumbs under the front little finger lines and pull them towards you.
– Do a Pindiki stroke with the lines behind the thumb (photograph 4).

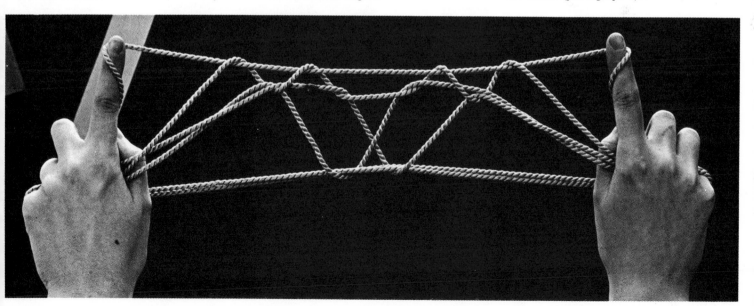

The Starry Sky

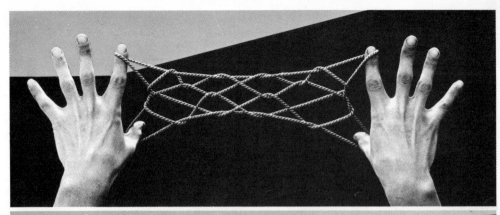

Photograph 1

1   Do opening A.

2   Bend the thumbs over the front crossed lines, and from above, bend them into the second crossed lines and pull the front little finger lines towards you.

3   From above, put the middle fingers between the index finger loops and the thumb loops, from below into the thumb loops, and pull the back thumb lines back.

4   Free the thumbs.

5   From above, put the thumbs into the index finger loops under the middle finger loops, under the back line and pull it towards you.

6   Free the little fingers.

7   With the thumb and index finger of the right hand take hold of the loop on the left middle finger, give it half a twist round in a clockwise direction and lay it around the thumb and index finger of the left hand. Do the same on the right; twist it half-way round in an anti-clockwise direction.

8   Do a Navaho leap over the index fingers.

9   Do a Navaho leap over the thumbs.

10   Press the lines which have just been passed over the thumbs down with the thumbs, and stretch out the figure.

First Variation (Photograph 2)

– Do first position 1.

– From above, put the right index finger behind the line running across the left palm and pull it up doing half a turn in a clockwise direction. Pull the string tight and do the same on the right.

– Carry out movements 2–10.

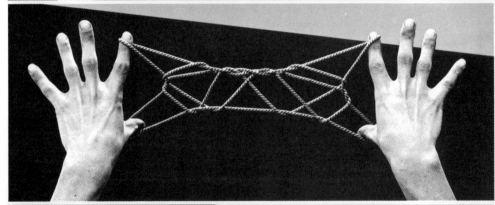

Second Variation (Photograph 3)

– Carry out movements 1 and 2.

– From above, put the middle fingers between the index finger lines, under the back thumb lines, and pull them back.

– Carry out movements 4–10.

Third Variation (Photograph 4)

– Do opening A.

– Bend the thumbs over the front crossed lines, put them between the back crossed

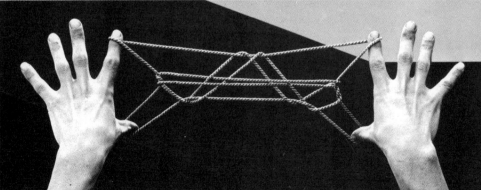

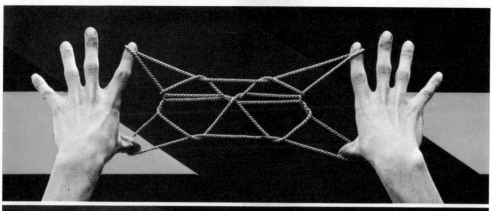

lines from below and pull the front little finger lines towards you.
– From above, put the middle fingers between the index finger lines, under the back thumb lines and pull these back.
– Carry out movements 4–10.

Fourth Variation (Photograph 5)
– Do opening A.
– Bend the thumbs over the front crossed lines, put them between the back crossed lines from below and pull the back index finger lines towards you.
– Carry out movements 3 and 4.
– Bend the thumbs over the index finger lines, middle finger lines and front little finger lines, put them under the back line and pull it towards you.
– Carry out movements 6–10.

Fifth Variation (Photograph 6)
– Do opening A.
– Bend the thumbs over all the crossed lines, put them under the back line and pull it towards you.
– Carry out movements 3–10.

Sixth Variation (Photograph 7)
– Carry out movements 1–4.
– Bend the thumbs under all the lines and pull the back line towards you.
– Carry out movements 6–10.

Seventh Variation (Photograph 8)
– Carry out movements 1–4.
– Bend the thumbs under the index finger loops and middle finger loops, over the front little finger lines, under the back line and pull it towards you.
– Carry out movements 6–10.

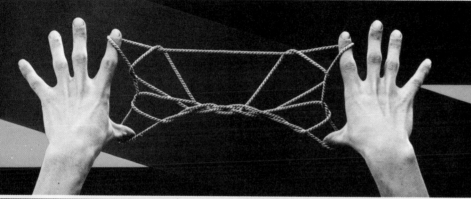

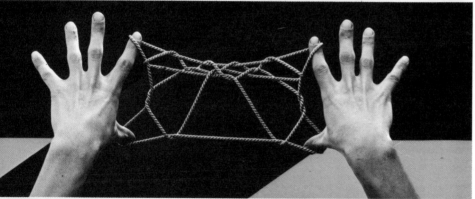

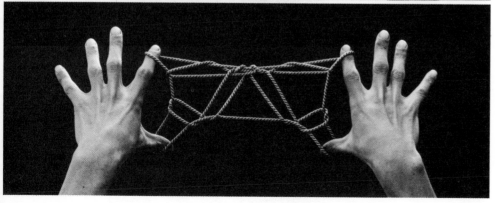

Two Coyotes

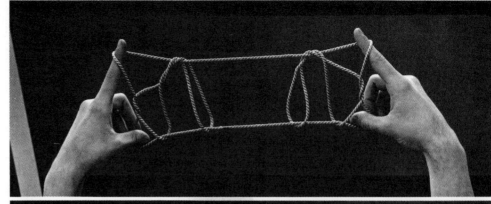

Photograph 1

1 Do opening A.

2 From above, put the thumbs between the back crossed lines, under the front little finger lines and pull them towards you.

3 From above, bend the middle fingers between the index finger loops and the thumb loops, under the back thumb line and pull it back.

4 Free the thumbs.

5 Put the thumbs under the front index finger line, over the back index finger line, under all the other lines and pull the back line towards you.

6 Free the little fingers.

7 Take the loop off the left middle finger, twist it half-way in a clockwise direction and lay it around the index finger. Do the same on the right, giving the loop half a twist in an anti-clockwise direction.

8 Do a Navaho leap over the index fingers. Let the figure remain slack.

9 From below, put the thumbs into the index finger loops and carefully do a Navaho leap over the thumbs.

10 Stretch the figure by pressing down with the thumbs on the line which has just been passed over, and pulling them outwards.

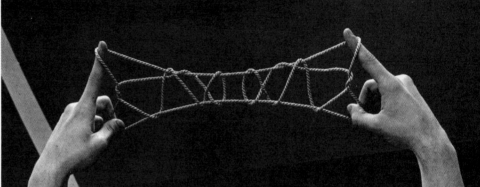

First Variation (Photograph 2)

– Carry out movements 1–4.

– From below, put the thumbs into the index finger loops, from above put them into the middle finger loops, over the front little finger lines, under the back line and pull it towards you. Carry out movements 6–10.

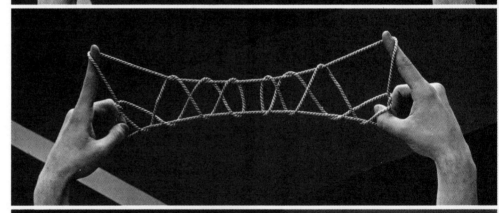

Second Variation (Photograph 3)

– Carry out movements 1–4.

– From below, put the thumbs into the index finger loops, from above into the middle finger loops, under the front little finger lines, under the back line and pull it towards you. Carry out movements 6–10.

Third Variation (Photograph 4)

– Carry out movements 1–4.

– From below, put the thumbs into the index finger loops, under the middle finger loops, over the front little finger lines, under the back line and pull towards you. Carry out movements 6–10.

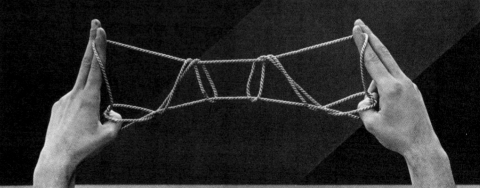

The Gated Well

Photograph 1

1 Do opening A.

2 Bend the index fingers over the back crossed lines, pull both these lines towards you with the index fingers bent over and stretch the index fingers back up between the front crossed lines.

3 Free the little fingers.

4 From above, put the free fingers of both hands into the index finger loops and press the back double lines against the palms of the hands.

5 Carefully free the thumbs, put them over the line which has just been released, on the outside behind the diagonal lines between the index fingers and the bottom of the figure. Take these lines on to the thumbs. Stretch the fingers to make the well.

6 Put the thumbs of both hands behind the double line just in front of the index fingers.

7 Do a Navaho leap over the thumbs.

8 Take all the fingers except for the thumbs out of the loops and let the figure hang down.

9 Put all the free fingers into the thumb loops from behind and stretch out the gate.

First Variation (Photograph 2)

– Carry out movements 1–4.

– From below, put the thumbs behind the bottom lines in front of the index fingers and do a Navaho leap over the thumbs on both sides. Carry out movements 6–9.

Second Variation (Photograph 3)

– Carry out movements 1–4.

– Carefully free the thumbs, put them over the line which has just been released and behind the bottom 'legs' of the crossed lines in the middle of the figure from the side. Pull these lines towards you and carry out movements 6–9.

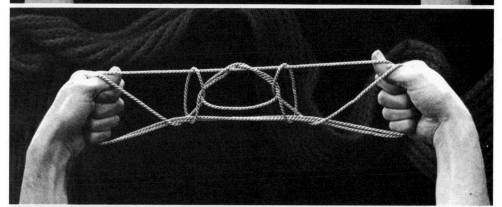

Third Variation (Photograph 4)

– Carry out movements 1–4.

– Carefully free the thumbs, put them over the line which has just been released and behind the top 'legs' of the crossed lines in the middle of the figure, from the side. Pull these lines towards you and carry out movements 6–9.

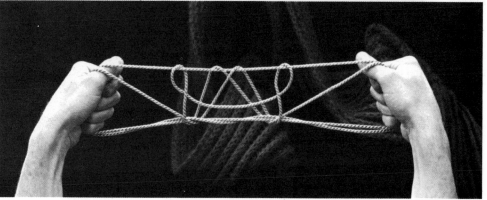

A Child is Born

An Australian string figure.

1   Do first position 1.

2   From below, put the right index finger behind the line on the left palm.

3   From below, put the left thumb behind the front little finger line and pull it towards you.

4   Bend the left index finger under the back thumb line and do a Pindiki stroke with it. Slide the straight line running from one thumb to the other on to the left thumb, under the line running from the thumb to the index finger.

5   With the right hand take the two lines off the left thumb and free the left hand. Put the thumb and little finger of the left hand between the two lines, take the back line on to the little finger and the front line on to the thumb. Pull the lines taut.

6   Repeat movements 3, 4 and 5 twice.

7   Repeat movements 3 and 4.

8   Free the right index finger and spread the fingers.

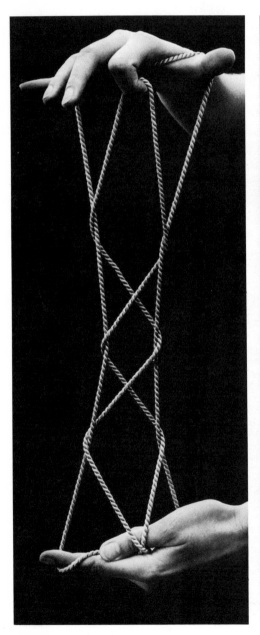
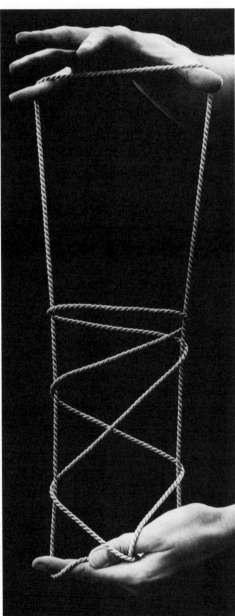
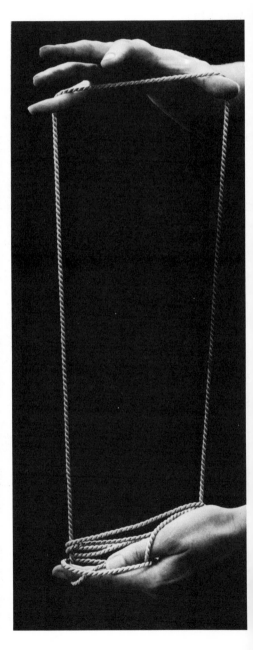

The Patamona Door

A string figure from the Guianas.

1 Put the left hand into the string circle and hang it from the wrist.

2 Take hold of the hanging lines with the right hand and pass the back line between the middle finger and the ring finger, and the front line between the thumb and the index finger of the left hand.

3 Pass both lines back between the index and middle fingers.

4 Lay the front line behind the thumb and the back line behind the little finger.

5 From below, put the middle finger and the index finger of the right hand behind the lines in front of the index finger and the middle finger of the left hand. Pull the lines taut.

6 Do a Navaho leap over the whole hand.

7 Slide the loops from the right index finger and middle finger on to the corresponding fingers of the left hand.

8 Do a Navaho leap over the left index finger and middle finger.

9 Slide the loops from the left index finger and middle finger back on to the corresponding fingers of the right hand. Turn the left palm up and pull the lines straight up (see photograph on left).

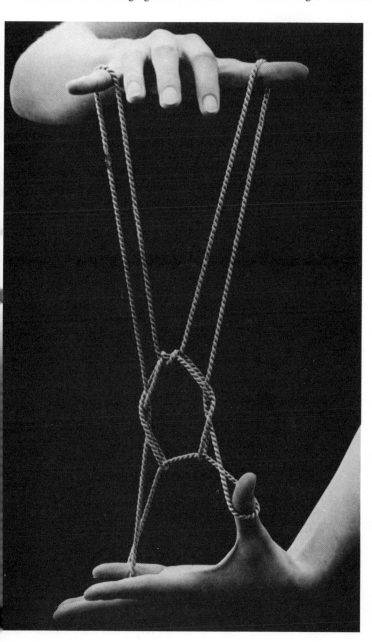

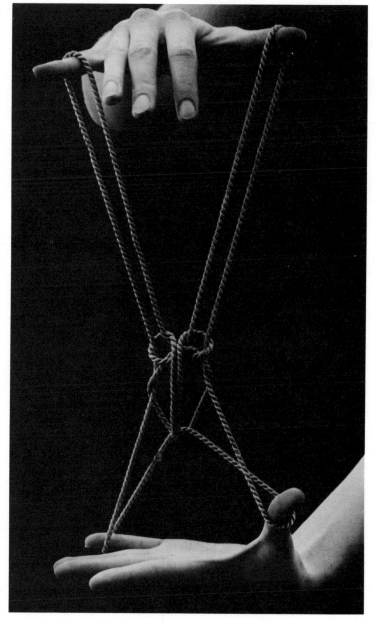

The Bat

Another string figure from the Guianas; see photograph on page 175 (right).
– Hang the string circle from the left wrist.
– Take hold of the hanging lines with the right hand and pass them between the index finger and middle finger of the left hand.
– Pass the front line back between the thumb and index finger, and the back line between the middle finger and ring finger of the left hand.
– Put the thumb over the front line, under the back line, and pull it towards you. Take the other line on the back of the little finger.
– Put the index finger and the middle finger of the right hand under the lower 'legs' of the cross on either side of the crossover and pull the lines taut.
– Carry out movements 6–9 of The Patamona Door (see page 175).

Climbing a Tree

A string figure from the original inhabitants of Queensland, Australia.
– Do opening A.
– Bend the little fingers over all the crossed lines, under the front line and pull it back.
– Do a Navaho leap over the little fingers.
– With the index fingers press all the lines in front of the fingers, between the index finger lines against the hand.
– Put your foot on the back line.
– Free all the fingers but hold the line on to the hand with the index fingers.
– Jerk on the string alternately right and left and you will see somebody climbing the tree.

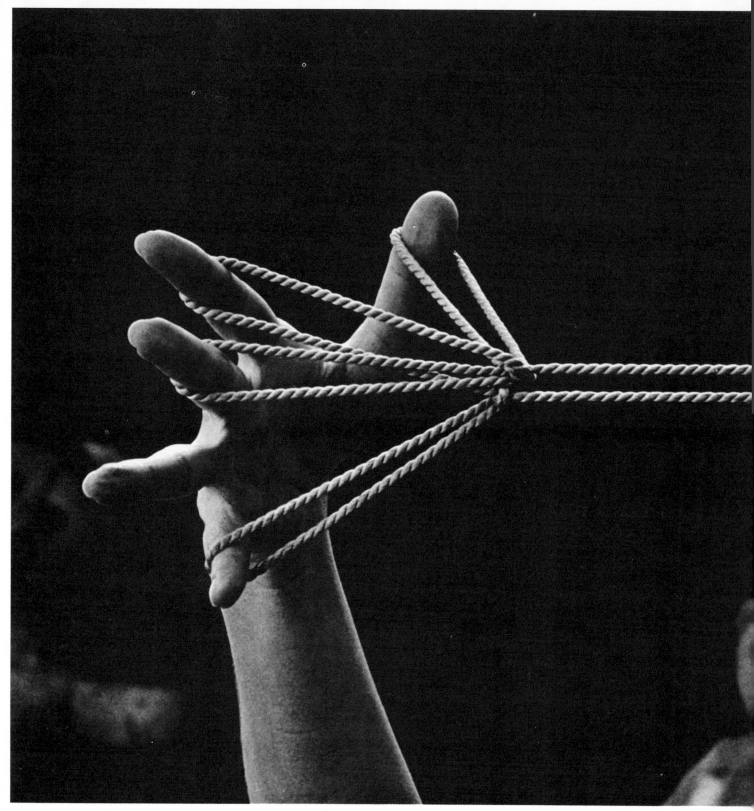

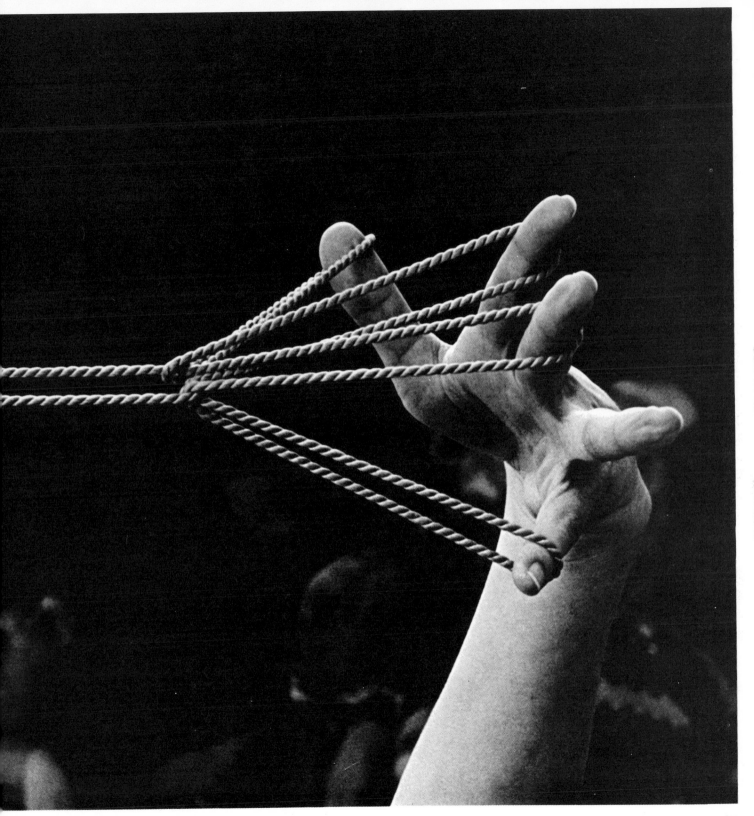

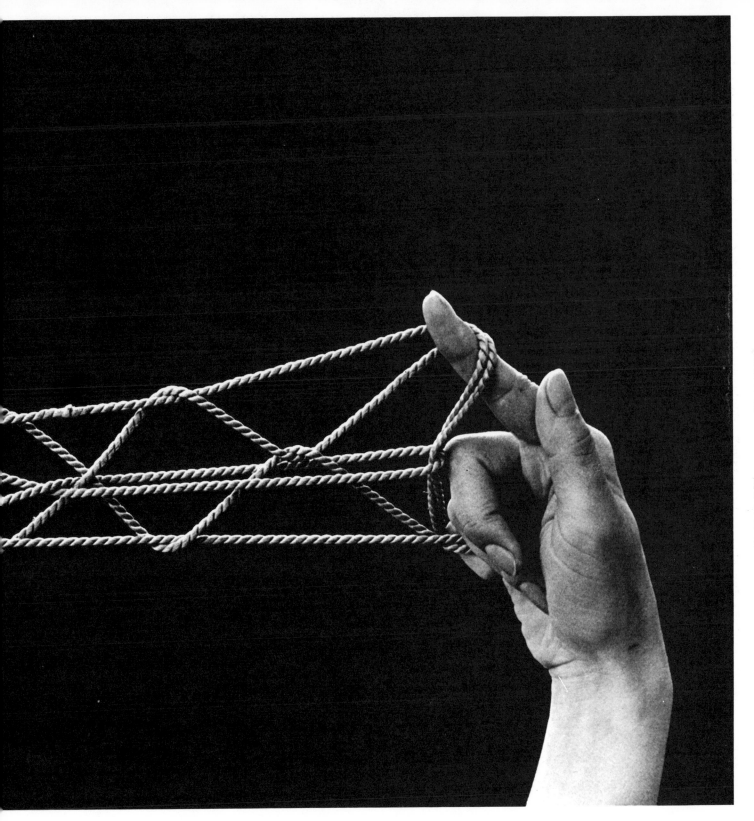

A Tree with Roots and Branches

This figure originates amongst the Indians of Guiana (see photograph pages 178–9).
– Do first position 1.
– With the right hand take hold of the line running across the left palm, give it half a twist in an anti-clockwise direction and put the little finger and thumb of the left hand into the loop from above. Do the same on the right, giving half a turn in a clockwise direction.
– Put the index finger and middle finger of the right hand under the bottom crossed lines on the left palm and pull the lines tight. Do the same with the right hand and stay within the lines of the corresponding fingers.
– Do a Navaho leap with the straight thumb line over both thumbs.
– Do a Navaho leap with the straight little finger line over both little fingers.
– Slide the loops from the left index finger and middle finger on to the corresponding fingers of the right hand. Pass the original loops from those fingers over them and slide them on to the left index finger and middle finger.
– Slide the loops to the fingertips and stretch the hands; hands one above the other.

Iburenio

An example of the complicated sort of string figures made on the island of Nauru. The name means 'A growth in the tomana tree' (see photograph on pages 180–81).
1   Do opening A.

2   Slide the loop from the right index finger on to the left index finger, pass the original loop on this finger over it and slide it on to the right index finger.
3   Turn the little fingers, the index fingers and the thumbs of both hands under their own loops one after another, first down and away from you and up again towards you.
4   From below, put the middle fingers into the thumb loops and pass them on to these fingers.
5   From above, put the thumbs through the index finger loops, then from below into the little finger loops and pull the front little finger lines towards you.
6   Free the little fingers.
7   From below, put the thumbs into the middle finger loops and pass them on to the thumbs.
8   Bend the four fingers of both hands over the index finger loops and the upper thumb loops and, from above, put them into the lower thumb loops; pull the front line of these loops up with the fingertips and then back, keeping the thumbs out.
9   From below, put the thumbs into the loops of the four fingers and take the four fingers out again.
10   Repeat movements 8 and 9.
11   Turn the thumbs around their own loops down towards you and up away from you.
12   From below, put the thumb and index finger of the right hand into the double left thumb loop, take hold of the front index finger line, pull it through the thumb loop and lay it around the index finger.
13   With the right hand remove the loops off the left index finger, put the left little finger into the double loop on the left thumb from below and pass it on to the little finger.
14   Lay the double loop you are holding in your right hand around the left thumb.
15   Repeat movements 12, 13 and 14 with the right hand.
16   Do a Pindiki stroke with the double lines running from the lines on the palms of the hands to the middle and free the thumbs.

The Dancer

A string figure from the Caroline and Loyalty Islands (see photograph below right).
– Do first position 1.
– Take hold of the front line near the left thumb and lay it one turn around the thumb.
– From below, put the right index finger into this loop and pull the string taut.
– From below, put the left index finger between the index finger lines, under the line across the right palm and pull the string taut. Do the same on the left hand, within the index finger lines.
– Free the left hand completely and let the string hang down from the right hand with the palm facing down.
– Lay the left loop (the one nearest the top) of the index finger over the right loop. Put the left thumb and little finger on the back of the right index finger between the two loops (at right angles to the index finger) and take the left loop on to the thumb and the right loop on to the little finger. Then take both loops off the index finger and pull the string taut.
– From below, put the index fingers into the thumb loops and pass them on to the index fingers; from above put the thumbs into the index finger loops and pass them on to the thumbs.
– From below, put the thumbs into the little finger loops and pull the front little finger lines towards you.
– Put the index fingers under the back thumb line and do a Pindiki stroke. Move the hands rhythmically and you will see why this figure is known as The Dancer.

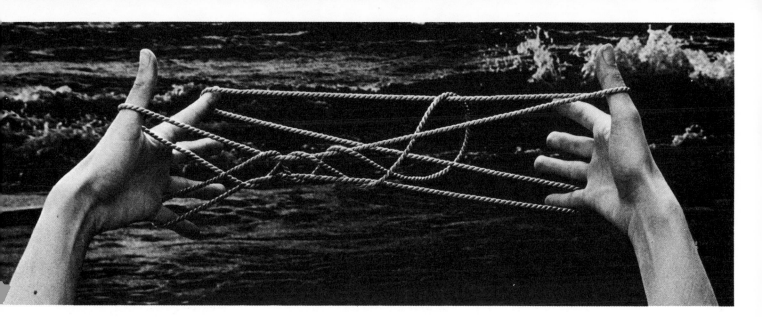

The King's Throne

A string figure from the Gilbert Islands where it is known as *Bao-n te nea*. It is also sometimes called The Bed.
- Do opening A and free the left index finger.
- From below, pass the lines from the left little finger to the left thumb.
- Carry out the following movements with the left hand three times in succession: Bend the four fingers over the top lines and pull the bottom line at the front of the thumb back with them. Now take this line off the thumb, and pass the loop lying around the four fingers on to the top of the thumb.
- Bend the four fingers of the left hand once more over the top lines and pull the bottom line in front of the thumb back with them. Extract all the fingers – except the little fingers – from the loop.
- With the left index finger lift the line running across the right palm: stay within the index finger lines.
- Free the right index finger and the king can sit down.

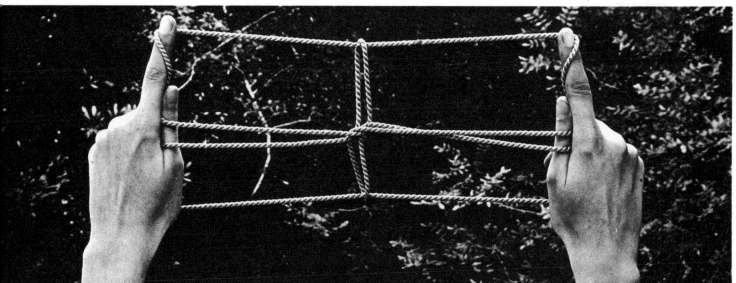

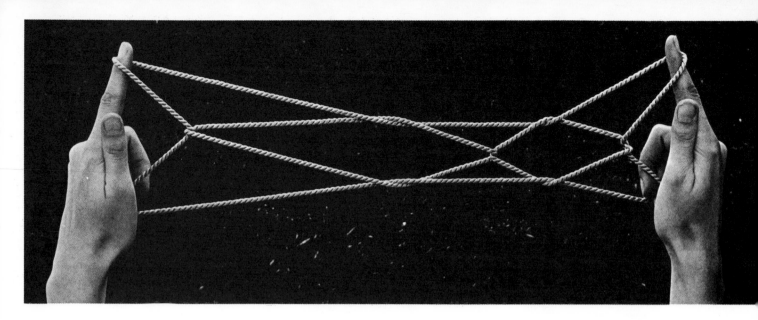

The Lizard

This Navaho figure begins with a variation on the Navaho opening.

– Do the Navaho opening, giving the small loop half a twist extra.

– Pull the crossover in the lines which are hooked together slightly to the right with the teeth.

– Pass the lines from the index fingers to the thumbs from below.

– Bend the index fingers and middle fingers over the top line behind them on both sides and secure the bottom line behind them between them. Pull this line up and turn the fingers away so that this line comes on to the index fingers with half a twist.

– Do a Navaho leap over both thumbs. Let the lines hang down loosely.

– With the thumbs, press down the line which has just been passed over the thumbs and spread out the lizard.

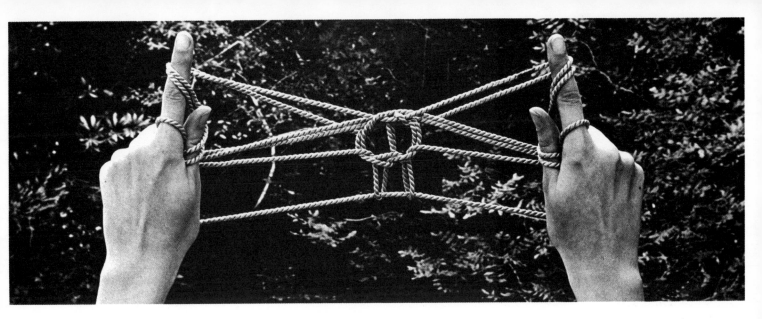

Mr Spider

A fairly long piece of string is required for this string figure from the Gilbert Islands.
– Do opening A.
– Bend the thumbs over the front crossed lines, put them between the back crossed lines from above and pull the front little finger lines towards you.
– Put the index fingers between the index finger loops and thumb loops, and from below between the thumb loops, and pull the back thumb line back.
– Free the thumbs.
– From below, put the thumbs into the top index finger loops and pull the index fingers out of these loops.
– Bend the little fingers over the index finger loops, put them into the thumb loops from below and pull the back thumb lines back.
– Put the index fingers between the back index finger lines and the front little finger lines and pull the front little finger lines towards you.
– Free the little fingers.
– From below, put the little fingers into the top index finger loops, pull them back and pull the index fingers out of the loops.
– Slide the right index finger loop on to the left index finger, pass the original left index finger loop over it and slide on to the right index finger.
– Bend the thumbs over the index finger loops, from below put them into the little finger loops and pull the front little finger lines towards you.
– From above, put the index fingers in the thumb loops under the front double thumb lines and do a Pindiki stroke with these double lines. Now you have an enormous spider sitting in front of you in its web.

Canoe with Two Sails

This figure comes from the Gilbert Islands where they say 'Te Wa Ma le-Na' as they do it.
– Do opening A.
– From below, pass all the thumb lines on to the middle fingers.
– Bend the thumbs over the front index finger line, under the back one and under the middle finger lines. From below, put them into the little finger loops and pull the front little finger lines towards you.
– Free the little fingers.
– Bend the little fingers over the back middle finger line, under the front and all the index finger lines and put them into the thumb loops from below. Pull the back thumb line back.
– Free the thumb.
– Bend the thumbs over the index finger lines, under the middle finger lines and pull the back middle finger line towards you.
– Free the middle fingers.
– Bend the thumbs over the index finger loops, under the front little finger line and pull this towards you.
– Bend the index fingers under the back thumb lines and do a Pindiki stroke (see the photograph on the left).

Kani Mumun

This string figure is one of a whole series which are used in funeral ceremonies on the Gilbert Islands in the Pacific. The name means 'dispersing clouds' or 'the flight of the conquered'.

– Do first position 1.
– Put the right hand under the line running across the left palm and pull the string taut. Do the same on the right.
– From above, hook the index fingers into the little finger loops, pull the front little finger lines towards you, put the index fingers into the thumb loops from above, take up the back thumb lines and stretch the index fingers. Free the thumbs.
– From below, put the thumbs into the index finger loops and pass them on to the thumbs.
– With the right hand lift the left wrist loop and lay it around the thumb and little finger of the left hand. Do the same on the right.
– Hook the front little finger lines on to the index fingers from above, pull them towards you, put the index fingers into the thumb loops, put the back thumb line on to the index fingers and stretch the fingers.
– Free the little fingers.
– From above, put the little fingers into the index finger loops and pull the front index finger lines back on the little fingers. Pull the index fingers out (photograph 1).
– Take the line which runs from one hand to the other straight through the figure, on the tops of the index fingers and do a Pindiki stroke (photograph 2).
– Free the thumbs (photograph 3).
– Move the hands apart (photograph 4).

The Fish

- Do the Murray opening.
- Put the thumbs over the bottom straight line, under the crossed lines and pull the lower back index finger lines towards you.
- Bend the thumbs over the top straight line, under the back index finger lines and pull it towards you.
- Bend the little fingers over the top index finger lines, under the straight index finger line and pull it back.
- From above, put the index fingers in the triangles next to the little fingers, take up the front lines with the fingertips and do a Pindiki stroke.
- Pull the little finger loops down and free the thumbs.

188

The Little Pig

In 1914 R. Compton discovered an amusing sequel to The Fish, on the island of Lifu.
- First do The Fish.
- Put the thumbs behind the outer lines of the 'W' in the middle of the figure and pull them towards you.
- Free the index fingers and pull the string taut.
- From below, put the index fingers into the thumb loops and do a Pindiki stroke.
- Go under the index finger line with the thumbs, bend them over the back little finger line, down and away from you and then up towards you.
- From above, put the right thumb and index finger through the left index finger loop, take the loop off the left thumb, pull it through the loop on the left index finger and lay it back around the thumb. Do the same with the little finger loop of the left hand.
- Do these last two movements on the thumb and little finger of the right hand.
- Take the loop off the left index finger and lay it around the left wrist. Do the same on the right.
- Slide the loop from the right little finger on to the left little finger and from the right thumb on to the left one. Take the right hand out of the loop.
- With the thumb and little finger of the right hand pass at right angles to the front under the left thumb, take the top loop on to the right little finger and the lower one on to the right thumb.
- With the thumb and index finger of the right hand take the two loops off the left little finger. Take the left hand out of the loop.
- Put the thumb and little finger of the left hand between the two loops you are holding in your right hand, take the front loop on to the left thumb and the back loop on to the left little finger.
- Pull the string taut and you will see the little pig lying flat on its belly. Put the index fingers into the little finger loops and pull the middle diagonal lines up. Now the little pig is standing up.

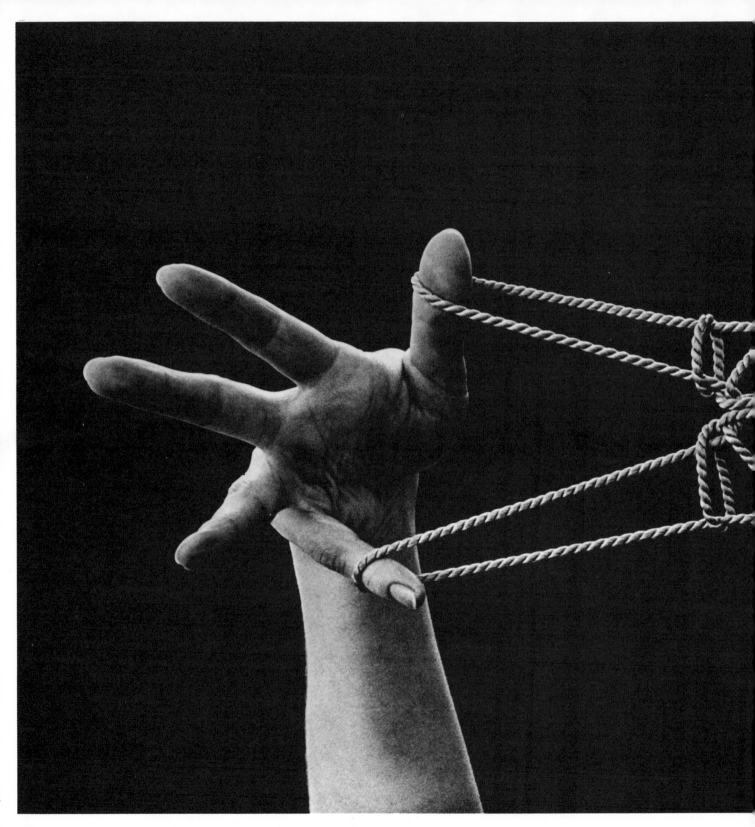

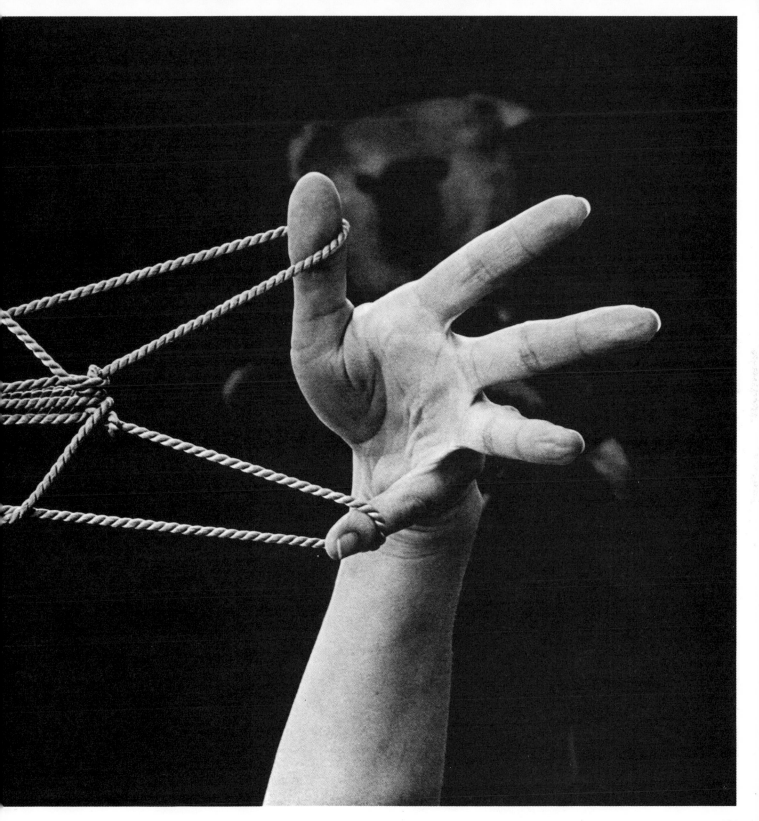

The Frog

This string figure was discovered in 1912 by F. Lutz among the Patomana Indians in British Guiana. See photograph pages 190–91.
– Do The Fish.
– Put the thumbs behind the double line which runs diagonally up from the index finger and pull it towards you.
– Free both index fingers completely.
– From below, put the index fingers into the thumb loops and do a Pindiki stroke.

– Put the thumbs under the index finger line, bend them over the back little finger line, down and away from you and up towards you.
– From above, put the right thumb and index finger through the left index finger loop, take the loop off the left thumb, pull it through the index finger loop and lay it back around the thumb. Do the same with the left little finger.
– Do the same with the right hand.
– With the right hand take the loop off the left index finger and lay it around the left wrist. Do the same on the right.
– Slide the loops from the right little finger and thumb on to the left little finger and thumb.

– Pull the right hand out of the loop.
– From the front, put the thumb and little finger of the right hand at right angles under the left thumb, between the two loops, and take the top loop on to the right little finger and the bottom loop on to the right thumb.
– With the thumb and index finger of the right hand take the two loops off the left little finger and pull the left hand out of its loop.
– Put the thumb and little finger of the left hand between the two loops you are holding in your right hand and pass the front loop on to the thumb and the back loop on to the little finger.
– Pull the string taut and the frog is there, poised to jump.

Silau, the Evil Spirit

This string figure was discovered and described by R. Compton amongst the Papuans on the island of Goodenough in 1912.
– Do The Fish.
– Put the thumbs behind the outer double lines on either side of the 'W' in the middle of the figure and pull these lines towards you.
– Slide the top index finger loop on the left hand on to the index finger of the right hand and pass the top loop on the right index finger over it; then slide it on to the left index finger.
– Pull the string taut and free the thumbs.
– Do a double Navaho leap with the two bottom loops of both index fingers.
– Pull the index fingers apart and let go of the index finger loops. The figure is hanging by the little fingers. Now put all the fingers into the little finger loops and you will see the evil spirit.

More figures

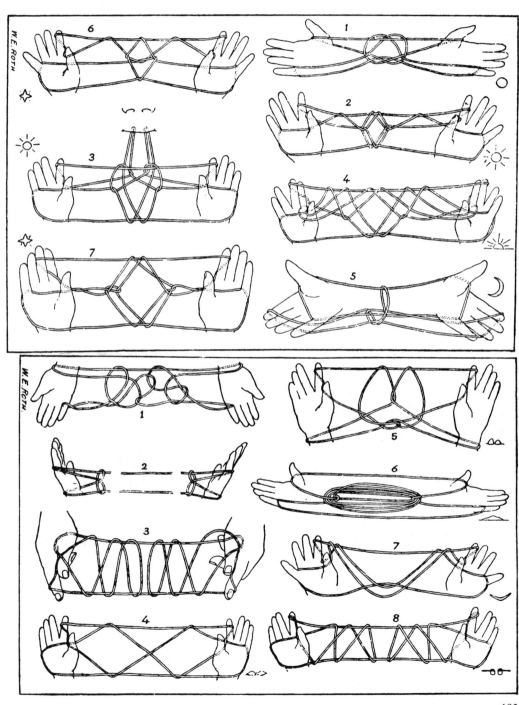

Illustrations from articles by W. Roth in
'North Queensland Ethnography', 1902.

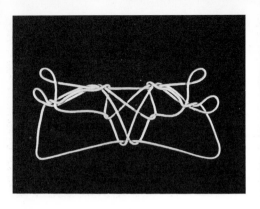

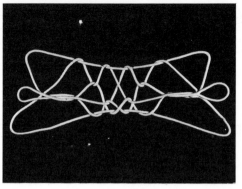

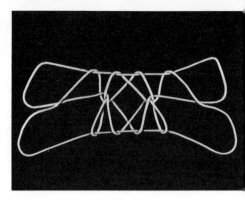

The Melon Rind

This figure originated amongst the Papuans on the Bamu river.
– Do first position 1.
– From below, put the right hand behind the line on the left palm and pull the string taut; do the same on the right.
– Bend the index fingers over the little finger loops, pull them towards you; from above, put the index fingers into the thumb loops, take the back thumb lines on to the index fingers and stretch these fingers.
– Free the thumbs.
– From below, put the thumbs into the index finger loops and free the index fingers.
– With the right hand take hold of the line from the left wrist and lay it around the left index finger. Do the same on the right.
– Bend the thumbs over the index finger loops, put them into the little finger loops from below and pull the front little finger lines towards you.
– From above, put the index fingers under the back thumb lines and do a Pindiki stroke.

Neneuri

The name of this string figure from the Gilbert Islands has never been explained. It is probably someone's name. You need a long piece of string.
– Do opening A.
– Bend the thumbs over the front crossed lines, put them between the back crossed lines from above and pull the front little finger lines towards you.
– Bend the middle fingers over the index finger loops, under the back thumb lines and pull them back.
– Free the thumbs.
– From above, put the thumbs into the index finger loops, under the middle finger loops, under the front little finger lines and pull these towards you.
– Free the little fingers.
– From above, put the little fingers into the middle finger loops, under the index finger loops and into the thumb loops from below. Pull the back thumb lines back.
– Free the thumbs.
– Bend the thumbs over the index finger loops, under the middle finger loops and pull the back middle finger lines towards you.
– Free the middle fingers.
– Bend the thumbs over the index finger loops, into the little finger loops from below and pull the front little finger lines towards you.
– From above, put the index fingers under the back line of the thumb loops and do a Pindiki stroke.

Ta Ai

This is one of the many string figures from the Gilbert Islands that are named after the sun.
– Do opening A.
– Bend the thumbs over the front crossed lines, under the back index finger lines and pull them towards you.
– Bend the middle fingers over the index finger lines, under the back thumb lines and pull these back.
– Free the thumbs.
– Bend the thumbs over the front index finger lines, under the other lines, below the front little finger lines and pull these towards you.
– Free the little fingers.
– Slide the middle finger loops up, bend the little fingers under them and put them into the index finger loops from above and into the thumb loops from below. Pull the back thumb lines back.
– Free the thumbs.
– Bend the thumbs over the index finger loops, under the middle finger loops and pull the back middle finger lines towards you.
– Free the middle fingers.
– Bend the thumbs over the index finger loops, put them into the little finger loops from below and pull the front little finger lines towards you.
– From above, put the index fingers under the back thumb line and do a Pindiki stroke. This is the first Ta Ai figure.
– Drop the twist around the index fingers.
– Free the index fingers.
– Put the index fingers under the back thumb line, do another Pindiki stroke with this line and you will see the final figure.

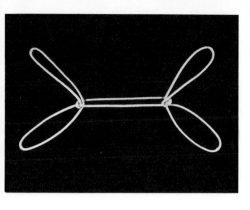
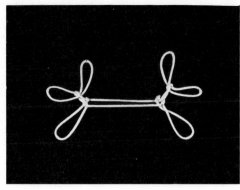
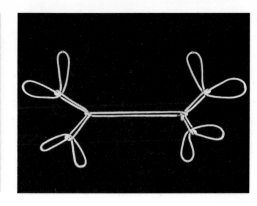

Crows' Feet

A string figure which is known by many different names all over the world. The feet can belong to an emu, or ducks or cockerels. It is sometimes called The Wooden Spoon or Two Tents. In England and Scotland it is known as The Lines of Lochiel's Dogs.

– Do opening A.
– Hold all the crossed lines securely with the fingers and throw the front line backwards over both hands.
– Put the thumbs behind the front crossed lines and free the index fingers.
– Take the line on the wrist on both sides and lay it around the middle finger.
– Pull the back middle finger lines down with the little fingers, bend the little fingers under the front little finger lines and straighten the little fingers.
– Do a Navaho leap over the little fingers.
– Free the thumbs.
– Spread the hands.
– These are the Crows' Feet (photograph 1).

The Pepper Plant

– Make the Crows' Feet, as before.
– Bend the thumbs under the middle finger loops and pull the back middle finger lines towards you.
– Take hold of the loop around the middle finger behind the front middle finger line of the right hand, bend the thumb over the middle finger line and put it into the loop from below. Do the same on the right.
– Do a Navaho leap over both thumbs.
– This is The Pepper Plant (photograph 2) that can go on growing (photograph 3).

– With the thumb and index finger of the left hand go under the front line of the left little finger, take hold of the back little finger line and lay it around the ring finger. Pull out the loop around the left little finger, over the front little finger line and put the ring finger in from below. Do the same on the right.
– Do a Navaho leap over both ring fingers.

This figure is also shown on page 120 with another piece of string woven through it.

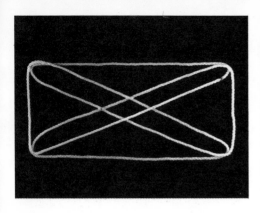 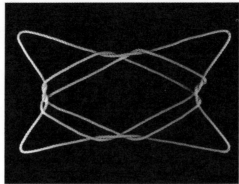 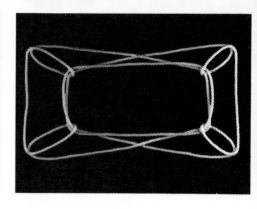

The Ace of Diamonds

A simple figure from Hawaii where it is called *E-ke-ma-nu*: the same figure as The Mattress in Cat's Cradle.

– Do first position 1.
– From above, put the right thumb behind the line running across the left palm, straighten the thumb and pull the lines taut. From below, put the right little finger into the right thumb loop and pull the back thumb line back. Do the same for the left hand.

If you continue this figure you get the last figure of Cat's Cradle, The Pig on the Pegs.
– Do a Navaho leap with the front line over the thumbs and with the back line over the little fingers.

The Big Star

A string figure from the Navahos in New Mexico.
– Do The Ace of Diamonds.
– Put the straight connecting line on top of both little fingers and then do a Navaho leap over both little fingers with the diagonal line.
– Lay the straight connecting line on top of both thumbs and do a Navaho leap over both thumbs with the diagonal lines. Pull the string taut.

You can now make The Hawk with another person by asking them to put their wrists in the little finger loops and putting your own wrists in the thumb loops.
See page 118.

The Rectangle

– Do first position 1.
– With the left hand take hold of the front line by the right thumb, take it in front of the palm of the hand, behind the little finger, between the little finger and the ring finger to the front, in front of the palm of the hand, between the thumb and index finger, behind the thumb, and let the line go.
– Do the same with the left hand.
– Do opening A with the bottom of the three lines on the palms of the hands.
– Go behind the front index finger lines with the thumbs, do a Navaho leap over both thumbs with the two bottom lines.
– Put the little fingers under the back index finger lines and pull them back.
– Do a Navaho leap with the two bottom lines over both little fingers.
– Put the thumbs and little fingers of the two hands into the index finger loops from below. Free the index fingers and spread the hands.

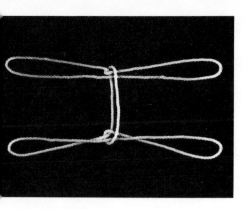

The Caterpillar

This figure is an extension of Crows' Feet.
- Do Crows' Feet (page 195).
- Pass the middle finger loops on to the thumbs.
- Slide the little finger and thumb loops from the right hand on to the left little finger and thumb.
- Bring the thumb and little finger of the right hand under the thumb between the two loops at right angles from the front.
- Pass the top loop to the little finger and the bottom loop on to the thumb of the right hand.
- Take the two loops off the left little finger with the right hand. Put the thumb and little finger of the left hand between the two loops and pass them over; the front one on to the thumb and the back one on to the little finger. Stretch the lines.

Two Coyotes

This string figure originated amongst the Navahos and represents two prairie wolves (see page 198, above).
1 Do opening A.
2 From above, put the thumbs between the back crossed lines, under the front little finger lines, and pull them towards you.
3 Bend the middle fingers over the index finger lines, under the back thumb line, and pull them over the middle fingers.
4 Free the thumbs.
5 Put the thumbs under the front index finger line, over the back index finger line, under all the next lines and pull the back line towards you.
6 Free the little fingers.
7 Take the loop off the left middle finger, give it half a turn in a clockwise direction and lay it around the index finger. Do the same on the right, giving it half a twist in an anti-clockwise direction.
8 Do a Navaho leap over both index fingers.
9 Put the thumbs into the index finger loops and carefully do a Navaho leap with the thumb loops.
10 Stretch the figure by pressing down with the thumbs on the line which has just been passed over the thumbs, and pulling them outwards.

Ussugdjung

This is the name given by the Eskimos of Baffinland to this string figure; it means either 'circle' or 'sun' (see photograph, page 198, below).
- Do first position 1.
- From below, put the index finger, middle finger and ring finger of the right hand behind the line running across the left palm and pull the string taut. Do the same on the right.
- Free the thumbs. Slide the string up on the little fingers.
- Bend the thumbs over the front line and put them between the crossed lines in front of the little fingers, and pull the front little finger lines towards you.
- From below, put the right index finger behind the line running across the left palm and pull the string taut. Do the same on the right.
- On both sides do a Navaho leap with the line behind the index finger, middle finger and ring finger – without pulling the lines taut – and the sun breaks through.

A Hole in the Tree

This string figure was described by G. Tessman who discovered it among the Chama Indians in north-west Peru. The same figure is found in many other places, especially Oceania. Its name varies considerably: it is known as The Sun and The Moon, as well as by every name anyone has ever thought of for the female sexual organs. This is the Chama figure (see the photograph on page 199, above).
- Do opening A.
- Hold the four crossed lines and throw the front line back over both hands. Stretch the hands.
- Bend the thumbs under the front two crossed lines (so that there is now a wrist line), press the back index finger lines down below the back wrist line and pull this line towards you on the thumbs, underneath the front index finger line.
- Do a Navaho leap over both hands with the wrist lines.
- Free the index fingers.
- Very carefully pull the figure tighter.

Darkness

A figure from Hawaii where it is known as *Po* (see the photograph on page 199, below).
- Do opening A.
- Turn the thumbs around their own loops, down towards you, and up and away from you.
- Turn the little fingers around their own loops, down away from you, and up towards you.
- Bend the thumbs under the index finger loops, under the front little finger lines and pull them towards you.
- Bend the little fingers through the index finger loops, under the back thumb line, and pull it back.
- Free the index fingers.

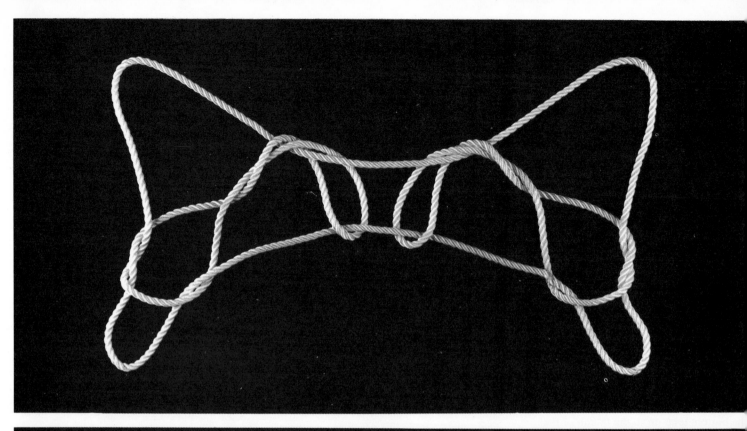

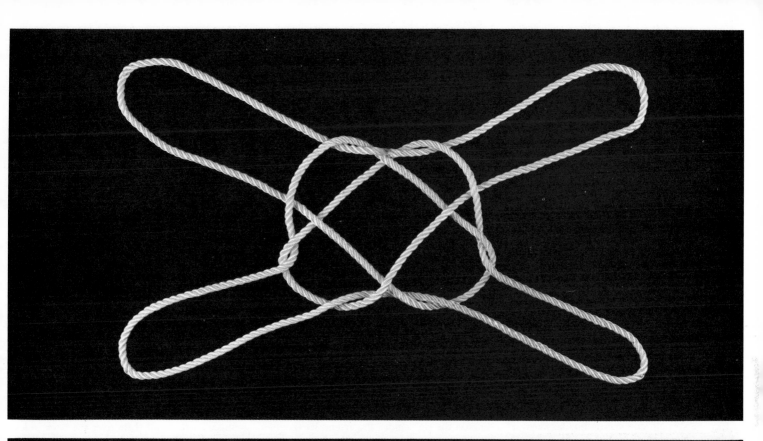

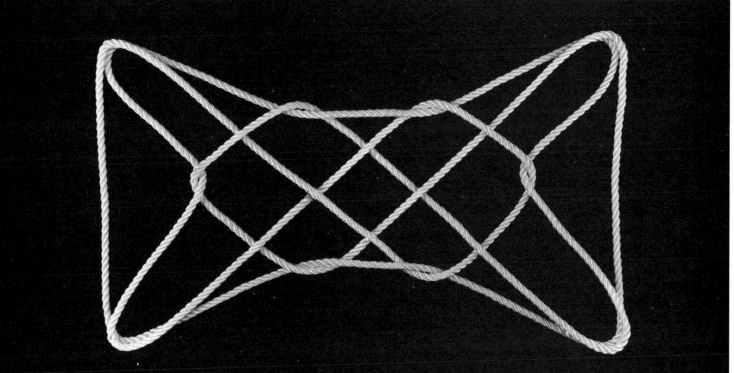

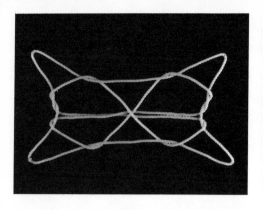

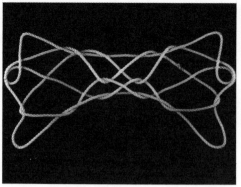

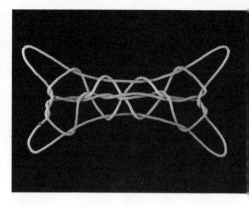

Carrying Bundles of Wood

The Navaho Indians carry bundles of wood on a head-band: the double line running across the middle of the figure.
– Do opening A.
– Press the thumbs and index fingers together on both sides, put them between the back crossed lines from above, under the front little finger line, and pull this towards you on both fingers.
– Free the little fingers and spread the thumbs and index fingers.
– Lay the straight connecting line between the index fingers on top and do a Navaho leap over both index fingers.
– Do a Navaho leap over both thumbs with the straight connecting line between the thumbs.
– Press the lines which have just been taken over the thumbs down with the thumbs and pull them outwards underneath. Spread the thumbs and index fingers.

Ten Men

This figure is fairly well-known on the islands in the Pacific and goes under various names: Ten Men, White Betel Leaf, Leaves of the Bread-fruit Tree and many others.
– Do opening A.
– Free the thumbs.
– Pull the back line towards you over the other lines with the teeth.
– Put the left index finger towards the mouth, over the left line, under the right line, and pull it to the left. Take the other line on the right index finger and let the string shoot out of the mouth.
– Put the thumbs under the index finger loops, into the little finger loops from below, and pull the front line towards you on the thumbs.
– Put the thumbs behind the top connecting line between the index fingers and do a Navaho leap over both thumbs.
– Let the top line slide off the index fingers.
– From below, put the index fingers into the thumb loops and pass them on to the index fingers.
– Put the thumbs under the index finger loops, into the little finger loops, and pull the front lines towards you on the thumbs.
– From below, put the thumbs into the top index finger loops and do a Navaho leap over both thumbs.
– From above, put the middle fingers into the small index finger loops and take the front line on to the middle fingers.
– Free the little fingers.
– Turn the palms away from you and spread the fingers.

Find the Owl

A figure from the Navaho Indians.
– Do opening A.
– Bend the thumbs over the front crossed lines, put them between the back crossed lines, under the front little finger lines and pull them towards you.
– Bend the middle fingers over the index finger loops, put them under the back thumb lines and pull them back.
– Free the thumbs.
– From below, put the thumbs into the index finger loops, bend them over the back index finger lines, under all the other lines and pull the back line towards you.
– Free the little fingers.
– Bend the thumbs over the index finger loops, under the middle finger loops and pull the back middle finger lines towards you.
– Free the middle fingers.
– From below, put the index fingers into the top thumb loops.
– Do a Navaho leap over both index fingers.
– Do a Navaho leap over both thumbs.
– Press the lines which have just been passed over down with the thumbs and pull them outwards underneath. Spread the thumbs and index fingers.

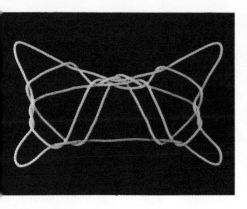

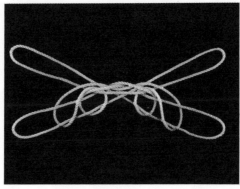

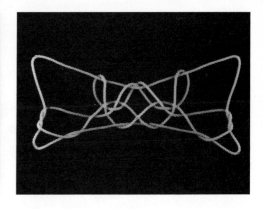

The Owl

The Owl – known as *Nasha* to the Navaho Indians – is very similar to The Starry Sky on page 122, but the end result is very different because it begins differently.
– Do first position 1.
– From above, put the top of the right index finger behind the line on the left palm, do half a turn with the index finger in a clockwise direction and pull the string taut.
– Do the same on the other hand; stay within the index finger lines and turn in an anti-clockwise direction. These movements take the place of opening A. Apart from this, do all the movements of The Starry Sky.

Two Dolphins

– Do opening A.
– Bend the thumbs over the front crossed lines and put them between the back crossed lines from above; pull the front little finger line towards you on the thumbs.
– Put the middle fingers under the back thumb lines and take them on to the middle fingers.
– Spread the hands as far as possible and lay the figure on your knees. Carefully take the thumbs out of their loops, without pulling the figure apart.
– From above, put the thumbs through these loops and under all the lines; lay the back line on the thumbs, carefully lift the figure and pull the line towards you on the thumbs.
– From below, put the little fingers into the middle finger loops and do a Navaho leap over both little fingers.
– Lay the index finger loops around the thumbs.
– Do a Navaho leap over both thumbs.
– Free the little fingers, pull the hands apart with a rapid movement, and the two dolphins jump out of the water.

The Cow's Head

This figure originally comes from the Navaho Indians and is also known as The Star with Two Horns.
– Follow the movements for the Two Coyotes (see page 197) up to number 4.
– Bend the thumbs over the front line, under all the other lines and pull the back line towards you on the thumbs. Now follow the instructions for the Two Coyotes from number 6.

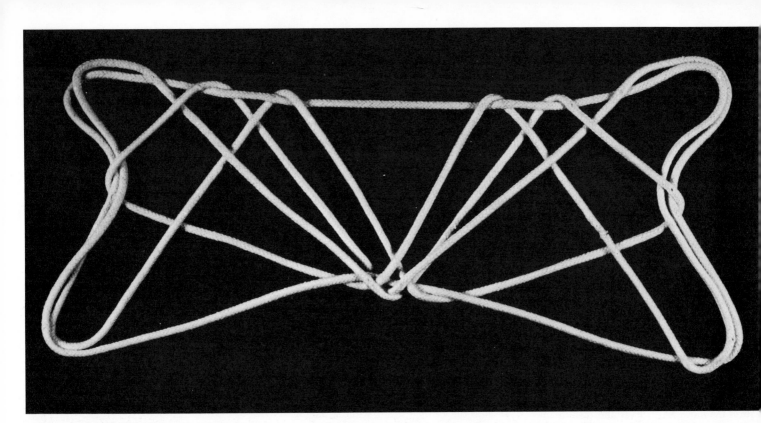

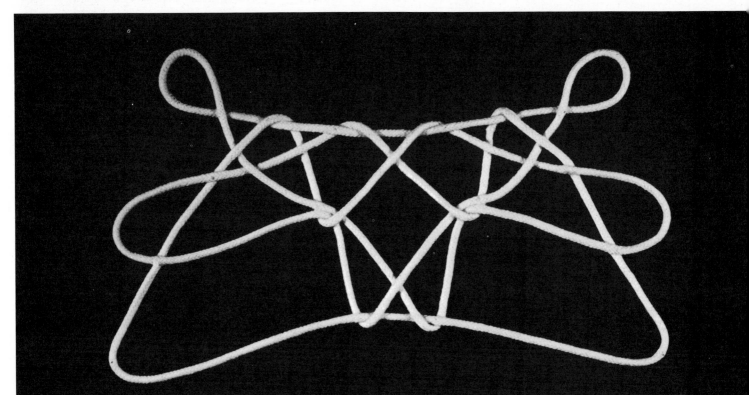

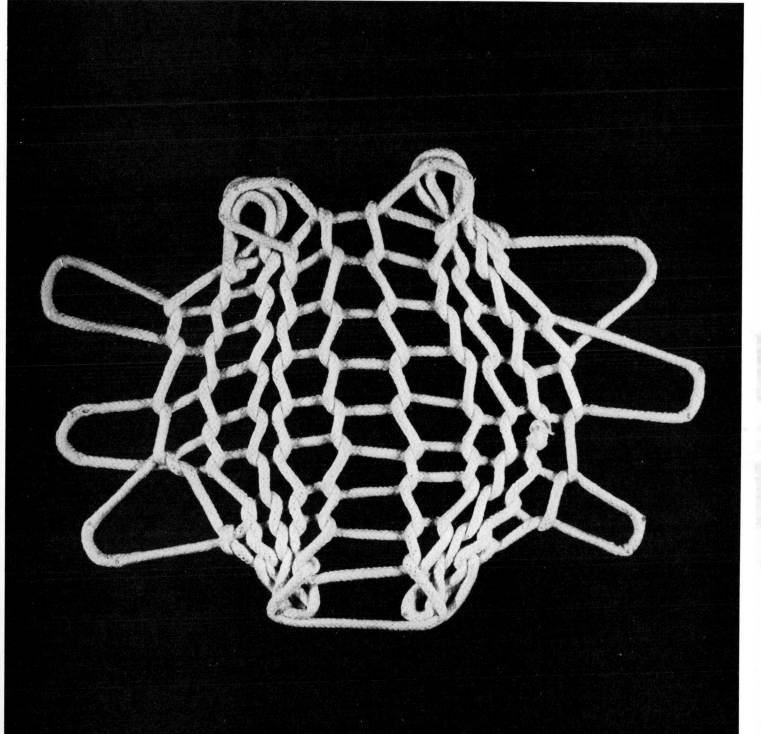

Rain

A string figure from the island of Nauru in the South Seas, where the heavenly waters are known as *O-eron* (see the photograph on page 202, above).
– Do opening A.
– Bend the thumbs under the index finger lines and put them into the little finger loops from below, over the back little finger line, down and towards you.
– Free the little fingers.
– From below, put the index finger and thumb of the left hand into the thumb loops of the right hand, take hold of the front index finger line, pull it through the loops and lay it behind the index finger. Take both back index finger lines between index finger and thumb off the right index finger, take the left thumb loops on to the little finger from below and put the thumb into the loops you are holding in your right hand.
– Follow these movements with the left hand.
– Do a Pindiki stroke with the double lines running straight across the thumb loops. Free the thumbs.

The Coconut Net

This figure is known as *Teibu Te Tatai* on the Gilbert Islands where it comes from (see the lower photograph on page 202).
– Lay the string circle around the wrists.
– Make a small standing loop in the middle of the front line (left over right), put the little fingers into it from the back and pull the lines taut.
– Press the front little finger lines down with the thumbs below the back wrist line and pull it towards you with the thumbs.
– Take hold of the thumb line with the teeth and take out the thumbs. Go round the mouth loop with the left thumb and pull the right mouth line to the left. Go round the left mouth line with the right thumb and pull it to the right. Let go of the mouth loop.
– Lift the wrist lines and lay them around the middle fingers.
– Put the thumbs over the middle finger loops, into the little finger loops from below and pull the front little finger lines towards you.
– Put the index fingers under the back thumb lines and do a Pindiki stroke.

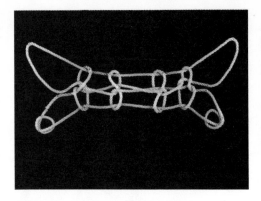

Four Boys
Hand-in-hand

A string figure which originates in Australia, and which needs a long piece of string.
– Do the Murray opening.
– Put the thumbs and little fingers between the top index finger lines from below, spread the hand and let this line slide off the index finger.
– From below, put the right middle finger behind the line connecting the thumb and little finger of the left hand, pull the string taut and do the same with the left middle finger on the right. (Stay between the middle finger lines.)
– Take the two lines off the left little finger, give them half a turn in an anti-clockwise direction and lay them around the left ring finger. Do the same on the right, turning in a clockwise direction.
– Lift all the lines off the left hand – with the exception of the front and back line – with the thumb and index finger of the right hand, go over the back line with the left little finger, under the bunch and under the front line. Then pull it back. Do the same on the right.
– Free the thumbs.
– Put the thumbs over the front line, under all the other lines, and pull the back line towards you.
– Bend the little fingers towards you and put them under the diagonal lines which are on top in the middle of the figure and pull these back.
– Do a Navaho leap over the little fingers.
– Take the loops off the index fingers, middle fingers and ring fingers on both sides and pull the figure apart a little.
– From above, put the index fingers into the

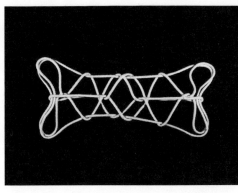

The Paths to the Well

A figure from the Gilbert Islands which is clearly similar to the complicated Nauru figures, especially Iburenio on pages 180–81.
– Do opening A.
– For the rest follow instructions 3–16 of Iburenio (see page 182).

thumb loops, under the front lines, and in this way pass the loops on to the index fingers.
– Put the thumbs – under all the lines – into the little finger loops from below, pull the thumbs towards you with the front little finger lines, and put them into the index finger loops from below. Free the index fingers.
– From above, put the index fingers into the thumb loops and do a Pindiki stroke with the back thumb lines. If necessary, pull at the figure to get a better shape.

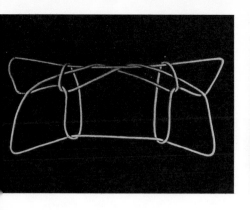

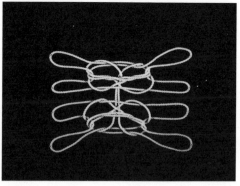

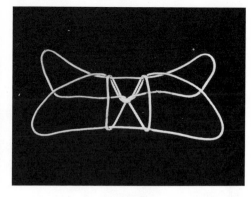

Two Wells

This figure is known as *Tan iti ran* on the Gilbert Islands where it originates.

– Hang the string circle around the wrists, make a standing loop in the front line, put the little fingers into this loop from behind and pull the string taut.

– Bend the thumbs down and towards you, under the front wrist line, over the back wrist line, down and away from you, and pull the back wrist line towards you.

– Do a Navaho leap over both hands (leaving the lines slack).

– Bend the thumbs under the front little finger lines and pull them towards you.

– Bend the index fingers under the back thumb line and do a Pindiki stroke.

Two Islands Linked by a Bridge

This figure comes from the Warau Indians in Guiana.

– Do opening A.

– Free the little fingers. From below, put the little fingers in front of the back index finger line and pull it back.

– Take the lines in front of the middle finger and ring finger on to the middle finger of the other hand, just as in opening A.

– From above, go behind the back index finger line of the right hand with the thumb and index finger of the left hand, under both index finger lines and take up the back thumb line. Then pull this under the index finger lines, then over, and lay it around the thumb. From the front, go under the two middle finger lines with the thumb and index finger, take hold of the front little finger line, pull it under both ring finger lines and then over them and lay it around the little finger.

– Do all this with the left hand.

– Slide the loops from the right index and middle fingers on to the corresponding fingers of the left hand, take the original loops that were on these fingers over them and slide them on to the right index and middle fingers.

– From behind, bend the index fingers under the straight line from one thumb to the other and pull it up with the fingertips, and take the thumbs out.

– Do a Navaho leap over both index fingers.

– From the front, bend the middle fingers under the straight line from one little finger to the other and pull it up on the fingertips. Take the little fingers out.

– Do a Navaho leap over both middle fingers.

Two Dragonflies

This figure is also from the Gilbert Islands where it is known as *U-oman ni keketi*.

– Do opening A.

– Bend the index fingers away from you, over all the lines, down towards you and above the back thumb lines, put them behind these lines from above and take them up on to the fingertips.

– Free the thumbs.

– From below, put the thumbs into the index finger loops next to the index fingers and stretch the loops.

– Do a Navaho leap over both thumbs.

– Let go of the top index finger loops.

– Bend the thumbs over the index finger loops, under the front little finger lines and pull them towards you.

– Free the index fingers.

– Bend the index fingers under the back thumb line and do a Pindiki stroke.

The photograph on page 203 shows The Tortoise; the instructions are on page 63.

Contributors

Hands
Alfonse Cox
Will Spoor
Casper Thiel
Geraldine Brans

Cas Oorthuys' photographs are used as backgrounds on pages 49, 87, 122, 123, 130, 131, 132 and 133

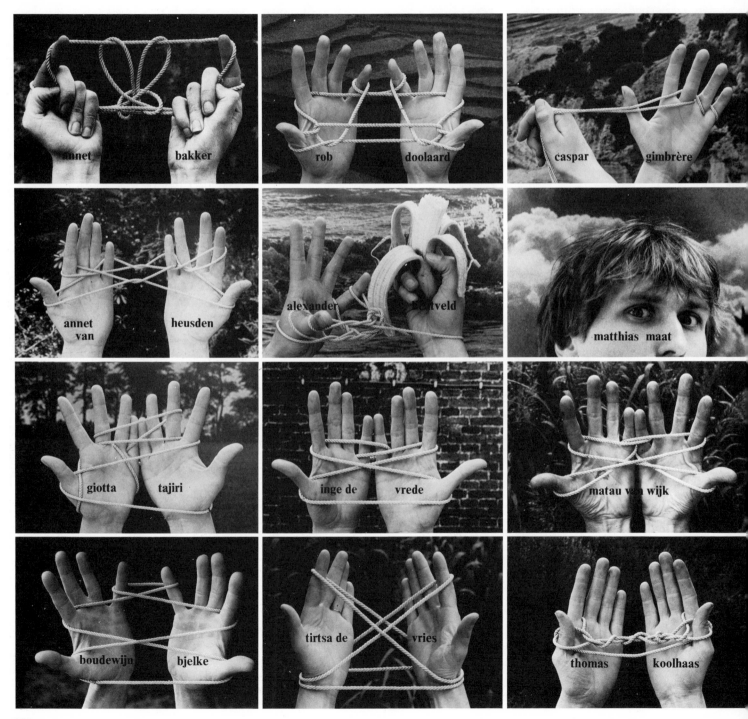

annet bakker

rob doolaard

caspar gimbrère

annet van heusden

alexander kontveld

matthias maat

giotta tajiri

inge de vrede

matau van wijk

boudewijn bjelke

tirtsa de vries

thomas koolhaas

In addition
we had the assistance of

Assistant photographers
Maarten v/d Velde
Eric Dix

System realization
Mathijs Theunissen van Manen
Boudewijn Bjelke

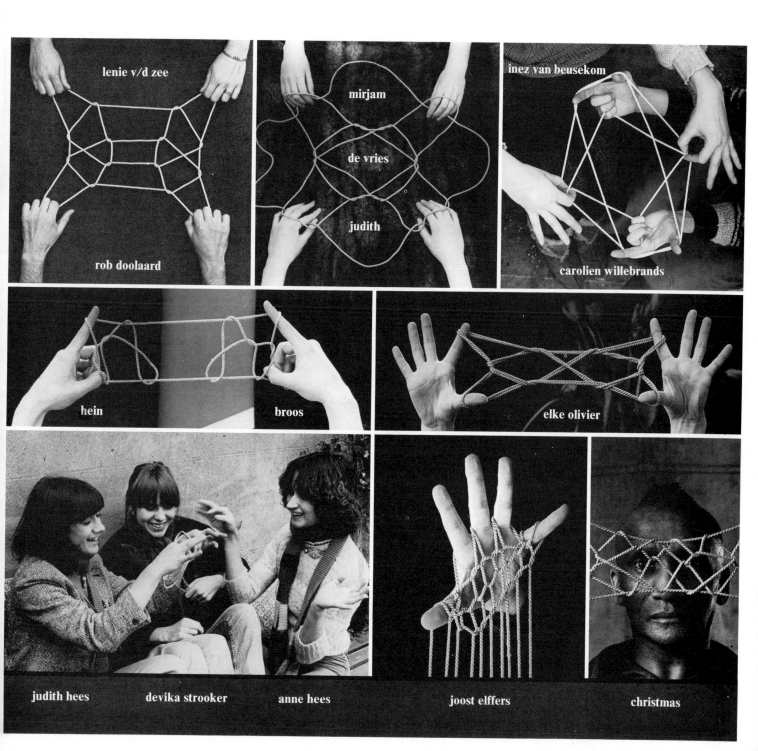

lenie v/d zee

rob doolaard

mirjam

de vries

judith

inez van beusekom

carolien willebrands

hein

broos

elke olivier

judith hees

devika strooker

anne hees

joost elffers

christmas